MAKE YOUR OWN
Board
Game

Designing, Building, and Playing an Original Tabletop Game

JESSE TERRANCE DANIELS

Storey Publishing

The mission of Storey Publishing is to serve our customers by publishing practical information that encourages personal independence in harmony with the environment.

Edited by Deborah Burns

Art direction and book design by Ash Austin

Text production by Liseann Karandisecky

Indexed by Christine R. Lindemer, Boston Road Communications

Cover and interior illustrations by © E. M. Engel Illustration

Additional illustrations by Ash Austin © Storey Publishing LLC, 29, 60, 78, 103 and Ilona Sherratt © Storey Publishing LLC, 38, 40 (board), 59, 61, 100, 111–113, 115 (all ex. characters), 116 (ex. characters), 119 (all ex. characters), 120–121, 125 (all ex. characters), 134–140 (all ex. characters)

Storey books are available at special discounts when purchased in bulk for premiums and sales promotions as well as for fund-raising or educational use. Special editions or book excerpts can also be created to specification. For details, please call 800-827-8673, or send an email to sales@storey.com.

Storey Publishing
210 MASS MoCA Way
North Adams, MA 01247
storey.com

Printed in China by R.R. Donnelley
10 9 8 7 6 5 4 3 2 1

Library of Congress Cataloging-in-Publication Data on file

CONTENTS

WHAT MAKES A GAME? 5

MECHANICS 19

GAME CRAFTING 105

To those who believed in me
when I forged my own path.

Thank you to my teachers,
Bonnie Tatro Capogna
and Patricia Galvis Assmus.

Thank you to my wife, Jaclyn Gladstein.

Thank you to my friends and family.

FOR THE GAMER IN EVERYONE

Make Your Own Board Game focuses on tabletop game creation. It takes the tricky terminology of game design and translates it into easily understandable language. Piece by piece, tabletop games are broken down into their most basic parts so that you can understand how the pieces work and use them to build your own game from the ground up.

This book is designed for the gamer in everyone. It's accessible to a younger audience, and adults will find it a useful resource. It's a handbook that focuses on design—not funding, publishing, manufacturing, marketing, or any of the less creative aspects associated with crafting a game. The first step to success is to focus on creating a game that is accessible, fun, and timeless.

This handbook is for aspiring young game designers. It's for the ones creating house rules in existing games and crafting together expansions by collaging homemade components. It's also for those who are attempting to produce brand-new games. It's for all crafters: from those designing their first game to pros looking to improve their crafting skills.

This book will strengthen your understanding of what makes a game great and illustrate how to facilitate fair gameplay. It explains the art of timeless replayability. It is a reference for gamers who want to use it as a collection of mechanics, explanations, and motivations. Even teachers who want to understand how to relay this information to students could use this book in their lesson plans.

CRAFTING A GAME

Gaming is full of educational opportunities. Players read and memorize; use math, logic, and deduction; gain social skills; bolster cooperation; and boost their creativity in a fun and interactive way. Game crafting is an artistic medium and an educational engine. Not only can crafting deepen your imagination and ingenuity, but it can also be enriching for the players. You may inspire players to wonder about strategy or create a game of their own.

Make Your Own Board Game will give you an understanding of the tools at your disposal. Just like understanding brush strokes and color theory before beginning to paint, or tempo and rhythm before playing music, the basics are the first step. Of course, you can pick up some drumsticks and start drumming. Maybe you're a natural! But it's important to study and practice; even the most naturally talented artists, in any field, learn about theory and style.

This book contains those theories, in an accessible format for all experience levels, but is especially helpful for those just starting. It displays a multitude of styles and interpretations in a practical order that you can easily reference. After completing *Make Your Own Board Game*, you can hit the ground running and create your very own games.

And not only will it make you a better game crafter, but it will also make you a better gamer once you have an empowered understanding of the construction, rules, and natural flow of a game.

NAVIGATING THIS BOOK

When it comes to gaming, a mechanic, also known as a mechanism, is a combination of components, rules, and gameplay, resulting in a process. It's similar to combining pulleys, gears, and screws to form a complex machine like an engine or a motor. A game is the culmination of multiple mechanisms, in the same way that many complex machines combine to create a car or robot.

This book has collected these mechanics into broad categories, such as what happens in a turn, or how pieces move around a board. Under each category, you will find examples of specific mechanics. Once you've digested the options available, you will be ready to move on to the Game Crafting chapter.

The Game Crafting chapter will show you where to begin and where you can go. Designers can craft games in millions of different ways—the creativity and original ideas you bring to the table will create a unique game.

The last section of the book provides customizable games to give you a starting point. These games are like a drawing reference that an artist uses to learn with their eyes and hands. Perhaps an artist is interested in sketching geckos. Without any geckos nearby, how can an artist know what they look like? A reference lets the artist cement an image in their mind and a muscle memory in their hand of how to draw a gecko.

The very same concept applies to this book's customizable games. They offer an example of a balanced game. The instructions provide the groundwork, and the customizations make it yours.

When you feel ready, you can craft games on your own. That's when this book will serve as a resource to help you figure out which mechanic will demonstrate your original game's concepts best.

Note that pink type identifies a term that will be followed by its definition.

Choose Your Own Route

If you're eager to get designing, feel free to start at the Game Crafting chapter. If you come across a term that you don't quite understand, use the index to find out where an example or explanation appears in the book. Jumping in with both feet, bounding around the text, is in the spirit of interactive stories where players make choices throughout.

WHY GAMING?

Gaming can be an excellent hobby for one, or a fun way to interact with friends, family, and people you've just met. It's an outstanding ice breaker for meetings, classes, parties, and just about any event.

GAMES COME IN A VARIETY OF SHAPES AND SIZES. They may require a board, cards, and props, or just your imagination. The term *tabletop game* encompasses all games that people can play on a table, on the floor, or in an entire room or space. There are many kinds, such as children's games, family games, strategy games, hobby games, indie games, designer games, Euro games, party games, and so on. All fall under the same broad terminology. Classic examples are Backgammon, Cribbage, and Charades.

GAMES TELL STORIES. Like a television show or a book, gaming can include a narrative from beginning to end, game start to game over. Each time you play, you get to contribute to a cooperatively told, ongoing epic.

GAMES USE VARIOUS FORMATS AND GOALS. You could be building a society, gaining currency, and properly allocating resources; or using deduction to identify a traitor or solving the mystery of a missing person. However you like to game, you are reaping many benefits.

Now you know why gaming is so outstanding, and why people play. There's a game out there for every type of player!

Interacting Socially ✛ Connecting Personally

Tactical Cooperation ✛ Healthy Competition

Utilizing Logic ✛ Reasoning Artfully

Exercising Imagination ✛ Fostering Creativity

World Building ✛ Achieving Goals

WHAT MAKES A
GAME?

Games tell a story through words, images, and interactions. Game design is a balance of patterns, shapes, numbers, colors, and abstract symbols. Let's take a close look at what makes a successful game work.

COMPONENTS

There are countless variations of gaming components. Here are some key elements you'll want to understand and become familiar with as you get ready to design your own game.

DICE

Many games have an element of chance. Unexpected, random outcomes change the course of the game. A die (plural: dice) is one of the simplest, most convenient ways to ensure randomization.

The six-sided die (d6) is the one most commonly used in games. The faces traditionally have small dots on them, known as pips, arranged in patterns signifying the numbers one through six. Gamers use many other unique dice, from the strange pyramid-shaped four-sided die (d4) to the 20-sided icosahedron (i-koe-suh-*hee*-drehn; d20) and more.

Or you could use a spinner, or spin wheel, with numbers or outcomes written on each "pie slice." Other methods of producing random results are to flip a coin and to pull labeled pieces of paper out of a hat.

Not all dice have pips or numbers. Some have images or icons. Players can advance a scenario or win a battle by rolling a particular symbol, a mechanic known as die icon resolution.

CARDS

Traditional playing cards have 52 cards in each deck, divided into four suits (spades, hearts, diamonds, and clubs). Each suit includes number cards ranging from 2 to 10, face cards (Jack, Queen, King), and an Ace, which can be used in different ways, depending on the game. Usually, decks also include a couple of Joker cards that can play various roles but have no value in the way that the other cards do.

Cards can come in a variety of sizes: for example, traditional playing cards measure 2.5 by 3.5 inches (6.4 by 8.9 cm); tarot cards are typically 2.75 by 4.75 inches (7 by 12 cm). The back sides usually display a single design on all of the cards within a deck. That way, players cannot tell which card they are about to draw. You can make them from paper or cardboard; experiment to find the right thickness for shuffling and heavy handling.

GAME PIECES

A game piece represents the player using it. It works best with a game board or tiles, so it has something to stand on, and often travels around the game board to accomplish a particular goal.

Game pieces can appear in a variety of shapes and materials, from folded paper cutouts to metallic statuettes. Miniatures are highly detailed and often painted by hand—a hobby associated with gaming. Meeples are traditionally wooden, designed in animal and people shapes, and come in a variety of colors. Figurines and pawns are other names for game pieces.

BOARDS

The game board is where the action happens—where the game pieces, cards, dice, and other components come together during gameplay.

Boards come in a multitude of designs, from simple line drawings to lush imagery—or artwork that's somewhere in between. They can be crafted out of paper, cardboard, or any number of materials, and they often provide paths for game pieces as well as locations for other components. The terms *board* and *map* are often interchangeable.

TILES

A set of tiles can be used as a substitute for a board or map. Players may start with a completed board of joined tiles or be required to build the board with tiles during gameplay. The tiles may be square, rectangular, or hexagonal.

Many tiles have specific traits or limitations. For example, in Dominoes, when tiles are laid, their ends must match. Other times tiles may provide a resource, or you may need to buy them before you can play them.

Gaming with tiles offers a unique experience every time you play because the way the pieces connect varies.

CURRENCY

In simple terms, currency is an item that represents a specific value. It does the same thing in the gaming world as in the real world. It can be an object, such as a plastic coin, faux paper money, or even just a number written on a piece of paper. And just as in the real world, in the gaming world you can gain, find, lose, and spend your currency. For example:

+ You can earn currency by reaching a specific goal or by occupying a particular space on a game board.

+ You can lose it to an opponent who has robbed you because a card they drew instructed them to do so.

+ You can spend it by purchasing a particular location or buying cards to add to a progressively growing deck.

Currency primarily represents money but can also be called something else, such as "energy" used to accomplish tasks. You could gain energy by resting, and then use it to buy cards that allow you to perform actions, as in the game Hibernation.

RESOURCES

A resource is very similar to currency. Both can be earned and spent in the same ways. One crucial difference is that a resource is usuallly a material, like corn, timber, or jewels.

Sometimes these objects require some form of labor. Using the examples given above, that labor would be harvesting, lumbering, or mining. Gathering resources then becomes part of a player's strategy.

A resource might be something general (like minerals) or specific (like iron ore); it depends on the game and its goal. With resources, designers can eliminate currency and embrace bartering. This can make it harder to pin down exactly what an item is worth but adds a fun negotiation element.

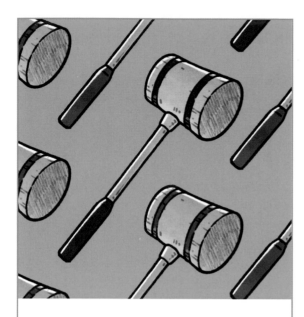

TOOLS

Some games have tools that the players use for specific tasks. A tool can be any real-world object, such as a small hammer to knock pieces out from the game board, or a key to open a chest. Tools can be a fun addition, allowing you to do something that you couldn't do with only your hands—just like in the real world.

Other miscellaneous tools could include a ruler to measure the distance between miniatures, or a pencil to mark on a scorecard. Even a magnifying glass or a decoder card could assist in searching for hidden clues on other components.

TIMERS

A timer's only job is to keep track of time. Some games require individuals to come up with clever words within a short period, while others ask players to work as a team, trying to escape a room as fast as possible.

Timers can come in many forms and sizes. "Sand timers" look like an hourglass and usually have enough sand for only a minute. Mechanical timers are dials that you rotate, with an alarm at the end. They are often constructed of internal gears and springs and don't require a power source of any kind.

TOKENS

Players use tokens to represent things that have happened during gameplay. For example, tokens may show ownership of a location, track points earned, or show that a player has sustained damage.

Tokens can take many forms, from glass beads to small pieces of painted wood or little cardboard cutouts. Games may refer to them as counters, markers, or even chits. A token or counter may even represent a character or a military unit, making them virtually the same as game pieces.

PROPS

Many games use props to create an immersive experience. It could be an immense volcano in the center of the game board, or a set of castle walls to represent a dungeon. Props could also serve a specific purpose, such as a map to display quest information or a type of terrain to signify slower movement.

Essentially, a prop is anything that the game could function without but that adds fun and flavor. Some may confuse a prop with a tool, but a tool is required to accomplish a task that cannot be done easily, or at all, without it. Some props simply make gameplay smoother, like a reference card that displays a list of potential actions and their costs.

RULES

 Rules are the bones of gaming: They tie together the ideas and components.

They explain plainly what a game is all about and what you are meant to accomplish. They contain crucial information, including a game's structure and turn order, as well as how to end the game, and how to win. The rules may also clarify specific situations and commonly debated issues.

Ideally, the rules (or instructions) create a fair and balanced playing field for all involved. They are like laws—you can bend or push them to their limits, you may find wiggle room or an innovative interpretation, but you cannot break them.

The rules are where you can find answers to your questions. They are the ultimate authority for the options and restrictions within a game.

There are two general types of rules: concrete and flexible.

CONCRETE

An example of a concrete rule would be:

"Draw a card at the beginning of your turn."

This rule plainly states that when your turn starts, you draw a single card. There is only one situation where this action can occur, and no other interpretation is possible. It is inflexible, and therefore, a concrete rule.

Concrete rules have less varied outcomes than flexible rules do. This leads to straightforward gameplay with fewer questions about the instructions.

PROS

+ straightforward gameplay

+ less-confusing rules

CONS

- less-creative gameplay

- can feel repetitive

Be sure of the kind of game you want to create.

FLEXIBLE

An example of a flexible rule would be:

"If a game piece moves for any reason, then its owner gains one resource."

This rule states that you gain a resource any time your game piece moves, for any reason. This situation can occur over and over for many different reasons, making it open to interpretation.

It doesn't tell you every way a game piece can move. This lets players find many ways to shift the game piece and gain more resources.

For example, a player may roll a die to step their game piece forward. Or they may play a card that moves their game piece to a completely separate position from where it was. Or an opponent may spend currency to send their game piece backward. For each of these situations, that player would gain one resource.

A flexible rule like this could be used in many situations and come into play many times in one turn. How flexible it is depends on the structure. Some rules in games are purposely vague to allow for a broad interpretation. Because flexible rules lead to many different outcomes, they can raise a game's replay value, with each session feeling unique.

Although flexible rules are fluid, they do have limits. You cannot manipulate them to fit any situation desired. They are specific and finite.

Be wary: Too much flexibility in rules requires a moderator, referee, or rule enforcer, also known as a game master (GM), to oversee outcomes fairly. Using a GM means that one person is running the show instead of interacting as a player.

Be sure of the kind of game you want to create.

PROS

+ unique gameplay with every session

+ more replayable

CONS

- rules could appear confusing

- harder for a new player to learn

- extreme situations require a game master

GAMEPLAY

 At the center of all the rules and components is the concept of gameplay. It's how a player interacts with a game. The rules say what you are allowed to do, and the components help you do it.

For example, if designers intend players to move a figurine around a game board, then they have to come up with a way for this to happen. Players may roll a die to move spaces, or they may play values from a hand of cards to move the game piece. The difference between those options is that one relies on chance and the other on choice.

How will players of your game take action? Will their fate be left to the roll of the die? Or will they create their own fate based on the cards in their hand? In its purest form, you can divide gameplay down to either a choice you make or a chance you take.

In its purest form, gameplay is either a choice you make or a chance you take.

CHOICE

An example of a rule that offers a choice would be:

"When you draw a card, add it to your hand. Then you may play any one card from your hand."

This rule allows you to decide which one card you will play on your turn. With the freedom to choose, players feel more in control of their actions. Plus, they can more easily adapt to situations and become more strategic over time.

If designers provide too many choices, however, then players could take too long to decide what they want to do. Players can become paralyzed by too many options. Do your best to strike a balance between giving enough choices to allow for the fun of decision making, but not so many that it's stressful.

PROS

+ promotes more strategic gameplay

+ increases control of your outcomes

+ provides room for improving skills

CONS

– can be difficult for beginners to grasp

– can feel stressful

– can slow gameplay because players take too long to decide

CHANCE

An example of a rule that relies on chance would be:

"When you draw a card, immediately play that card."

This rule forces you to use the first card that you draw. The card you receive is left up to fate. Rules that rely on chance let beginners and pros have a more balanced interaction since you're unable to know the outcome. People also require less of an explanation to start playing.

As a game designer, you can use chance in many ways: rolling dice, spinning a wheel, flipping a coin, or any other method of randomization you can dream up. In some games, players can try to curb the randomness: for example, by building a strong deck that will deliver what's needed.

Chance outcomes are more straightforward than choice outcomes. If a game relies too heavily on chance, however, players won't be able to improve their skills or alter the outcome, which can be frustrating.

PROS

+ clearer rules that are easier to understand

+ balanced interactions between veterans and newbies

CONS

– can be difficult to improve at the game

– can feel boring or frustrating with few or no choices

BIG-PICTURE DECISIONS

A game requires structure. This can occur in different ways:

+ A standard **competitive** game where players independently seek victory against one another

+ A **cooperative** game where players work as a team to reach a goal together

+ A **solo** game where a player faces challenges alone, sometimes racing against a timer

Shoot the Moon

It takes a balance of choices and chances to create an exceptional game. It's a lot like life: you're in control of many aspects, but not everything. Sometimes chance plays a role. All you can do is set yourself up as best as possible with your choices and, hopefully, receive a little good fortune by chance.

Of course, a significant difference between games and life is that we do not all receive a fair and balanced start. But don't let that restrict you, in games or in life! As they say, shoot for the moon, land among the stars.

Not only is shooting the moon a courageous effort but it's also the name of a particular move in gaming. To "shoot the moon" means that you're trying to reverse a negative situation and transform it into a bold, positive outcome.

For example, in the card game Hearts, the goal is to collect the fewest heart cards.

Each is worth 1 point, and in every turn, players try to avoid collecting any points.

If, however, you manage to collect every heart card, along with the dreaded 13-point Queen of Spades, then the result is completely flipped from negative to positive. Depending on the version of Hearts you're playing, there's one of two outcomes:

- Every other player receives those points instead of you;
- Or you get to subtract those points from your total score instead of adding them.

That's shooting the moon! Accept the negativity that you must, because one cannot control every aspect of gaming or of life, and resolve to be more positive than ever in the end.

Shoot for the moon . . .
land among the stars.

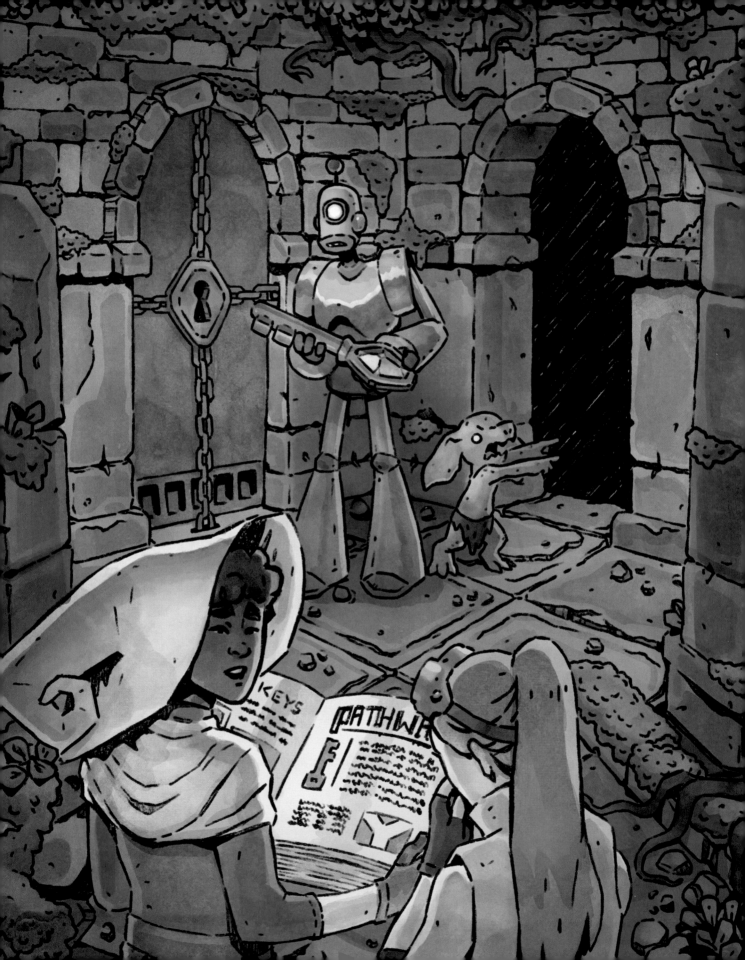

MECHANICS

Also referred to as mechanisms, mechanics combine the what and how of rules and gameplay to form consistent types of gaming, performing recognizable tasks from game to game. They are universal terms that describe how a game is played, so that a broad audience can easily understand, use, and discuss them.

HOW GAMING RESEMBLES SPORTS

If you were to compare gaming mechanics to sports, the idea of hitting a ball could be considered a mechanic. But, the instructions of what you must specifically do (rules), what equipment you use (components), and how you go about it (gameplay) differ depending on the sport.

For example, in baseball:

+ Players hit a ball, but the **rules** say you must do so while standing at home plate after being pitched that ball.

+ Players must use a batting helmet and a baseball bat—the **components**.

+ The **gameplay** requires that you wait for the perfect pitch and then strike the ball any distance forward (with limitations for foul balls), so that you can quickly make it to a base before your opponent can recover the ball and send it there first.

Hitting the ball is the basic mechanic behind all of it, but if you were to transfer that mechanic to a different sport, such as soccer, the way the entire scenario plays out is drastically different. This is how mechanisms travel from game to game, remaining fresh with alternate rules, components, and gameplay.

This chapter describes what kind of rules you can devise, how the gameplay might unfold, and which components might best represent each mechanic. It provides references to classic games and invented concepts as examples.

It's important to become familiar with all the described mechanics so that when you're ready to craft, you can quickly remember what might work best for your concept or theme.

Some terms used in this chapter are generalized for a more straightforward explanation, while others may be mashed-up and reestablished to teach the ideas more easily. Many books before this one have tried to institute labels on gaming mechanics and terms. This chapter simply takes what has been and what is, and suggests what could be.

As the designer, your structure of turn order should be based on the game type and mindful of the chosen audience.

PLAYER 1

PLAYER 2

TURN ORDER

In a competitive game, you face off against opponents and there can be only one winner. In a cooperative game, players work together in a team to complete shared objectives. Either way, the only time you can perform actions and accomplish tasks is when you have the opportunity to do so—on your turn.

Using a fixed turn order in a competitive game is the most typical and straightforward way of playing. Gamers select someone to go first and then take turns moving around the table. They establish the turn order at the game's start and stick with it throughout.

It's easy to see why turn order is considered one of the most essential mechanics in gaming: All players deserve an equal opportunity to take a chance or make a choice. This does not mean, however, that turn order is always played out in traditional ways.

CLASSIC GAMING EXAMPLE
Tic-Tac-Toe

A simple game for two players, Tic-Tac-Toe uses a fixed turn order and only a single action. During each turn, players leave their assigned mark (an "X" or an "O") on an empty space within a 3×3 square grid. By marking a space they own it, and the goal is to arrange three of their marks in a line.

Also known as Noughts and Crosses, Tic-Tac-Toe pits two players against one another. This dynamic is one of the most common types of gameplay—multiplayer games of opposition (competitive games).

SPACE COMBAT

Tic-Tac-Toe is a spatial game of positioning. Other spatial games may require that players arrange their components in certain ways or try to occupy the most territory. Spatial games will be further discussed in reference to area control.

FLIP to pg. 60 for more info!

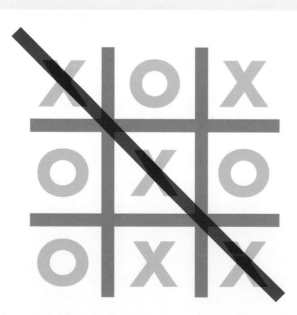

Tic-Tac-Toe is a basic example of a competitive game.

ORDER OF OPERATIONS

A game's flow and fairness depend on following the steps within each turn and keeping to the proper order of operations. In more complex games, turn order often includes multiple phases that tell you when and how actions can be performed.

SEQUENTIAL TURNS. One player goes through all the stages of their turn, in precise order, and then passes to the next player. Multiple steps can exist within a turn. This is a classic order of operations.

Example: Go Fish. Each turn, players acquire a card either from an opponent or by drawing one. If they get what they are looking for, then they repeat that step. They can also lay down any sets of matches they obtain as they come across them. It is simple and clear as to who is currently playing (the active player).

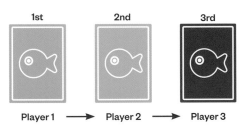

After the last player has taken their turn, order resets with the first player.

STAGGERED TURNS. All players go through the first phase of a round, in order, before moving onto the next one. Then they will go through the second phase of a round, before all players move on to the third phase, and so on. In simplest terms, each player can take a turn within a phase, and there may be multiple phases within a round.

Example: Poker. All players take a turn placing a bet in the first phase before progressing (moving on) to the second phase.

ALL PLAYERS PLACE A BET IN PHASE ONE

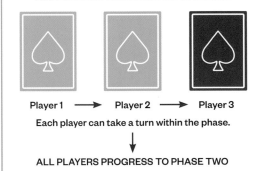

Each player can take a turn within the phase.

ALL PLAYERS PROGRESS TO PHASE TWO

Is It a Turn or a Round?

A turn is taken by a single player or team, while a single round is when every player or team has taken one turn. Ultimately, every player should get a turn before the next round can begin.

Some turns and phases can also exist outside of regularly occurring rounds, like a phase that is a precursor to the entire game. At the beginning of Charades, for example, all players simultaneously come up with ideas that they write down on paper and throw into a hat to be pulled out later.

ALTERNATING TURN ORDERS

Some games alternate the turn order every round. The mechanics that cause these changes are known, appropriately, as alternating turn orders, and there are many ways in which they can occur.

Whichever one you pick, keep an eye out for unwieldy methods that slow down gameplay. Also, it's wise to use a token that players can pass at the beginning of each round to signify who goes first. Alternating turn orders are discussed further in reference to action drafting.

FLIP to pg. 31 for more info!

RANDOM. A die roll or other "randomizer" determines who goes first. This structure can feel a little chaotic, because in every round the players must rely on a die roll to place them in the turn order.

I'M FIRST!

STAT-BASED. A player's stats, such as points, resources, or currency, determine who goes first each round. This way, players who work hard in one turn are rewarded by going first in the next.

I HAVE THE MOST! I'M FIRST!

BID. As in any auction, players bid on turn-order priority, before starting each round. Although bidding adds an element of excitement, it can feel like a punishment. New gamers may pay far too much or too little during the auction and waste valuable assets.

I'M FIRST!

PROGRESSIVE. Players rotate who goes first through a balanced progression around the table. For example, in Round 1, Player 1 goes first, then in Round 2, Player 2 goes first. This pattern continues until the game's conclusion.

Round	1	2	3
Player that goes first in the round	1	2	3
Round	4	5	6
Player that goes first in the round	1	2	3

Switching Up the Turn Order

Game designers should be cautious whenever they deviate from the classic fixed turn order. Using an alternating turn order can cause a lot of confusion for players and should be thoroughly tested. When applied properly, however, switching up the turns can create highly enjoyable and original gaming experiences.

As a designer, it's up to you. Games should aim at being fun and inclusive. All that it takes is a competitive spirit or some creative energy.

PLAYER JUDGE

Each turn in a game may play out very differently, depending on the active player. An excellent example would be games with a player judge. Usually, in games like these, the non-judge players are simultaneously performing an action in hopes of a particular outcome. But, ultimately, the player judge's decision determines what happens next.

Back-to-back turns play out very differently, since the judge's decision is dependent upon the other players' choices. For example:

+ A card is drawn from a shuffled deck and placed where all can see. The cards used have either images or text on them.

+ Next, the non-judge players simultaneously take their turn, choosing which card from their hand works together best with this drawn card. Often, this player judge mechanic is used in party games where the goal is humor. This means that non-judge players are selecting cards from their hand that match up with the drawn card in some humorous combination.

+ Then the player judge gets a turn to decide which of those cards presented by the players ultimately works best with the drawn card. It's as if the cards offered by the non-judge players have now become the judge's hand to choose from.

+ The player whose card gets selected then receives points or a benefit of sorts as a reward.

Usually, at the end of the round, the role of the judge will rotate to a different player, manipulating the turn order and allowing other players a chance to judge.

The player judge's decision determines what happens next.

TURN ORDER BY THE CLOCK

Time itself can define a turn. For example, all players could race against one another in real time to complete a task as rapidly as possible. This process doesn't have to take up the entire game; it may consist of only a single phase, after which turn order could be restored.

Traditionally, players use a timer as a way of ending the current phase. Other ways include one player completing a task before others or a deck of cards running out.

Other exciting mechanics that manipulate turn order include role order and action speeds, which are discussed in the section on simultaneous action selection. These mechanics use actions with priority numbers, or speeds, to determine the turn order.

FLIP to pg. 72 for more info!

ELAPSED REAL TIME. Players must end the game once a specific amount of time has passed.

TIME TRACK. Players move game pieces along a physical path, but the movement doesn't represent moving through space in the game. It represents the passage of time.

Players move forward on the track, often loosely based on how long actions take in real time.

For example, 50 minutes = 5 spaces.

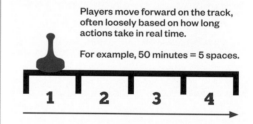

PUNCTUATED REAL TIME. Players have the chance to temporarily press *pause* on the clock and resolve particular actions. This changes the mood from hastily racing in one instant to thoughtfully contemplating in the next. Not only that, but it also provides a moment for players to take a break. Intensive real-time competition can be tiring!

Who Goes First?

Deciding on who gets to go first when starting a new game is a fun aspect of designing. What would make the most sense for your game? What best matches the theme or overall feel? How do you decide on the starting player?

If you're crafting a game about turtles, perhaps whoever is last to the table gets to play first, starting off the game. This would be thematic since turtles are slow, and it could turn into a hilarious pregame phase where players approach the board as slowly as possible.

Mechanics

26

LOSING A TURN

It's possible that every player may not get a turn in a round because someone or something makes them lose a turn. This could be as simple as someone playing a card that skips the next player, or landing on a space that forces them to remain there for the next round.

Sometimes the turn order can be reversed, too, sending it back the way it came. This process can cause players to miss out on their turn until the rotation comes all the way back around. Losing a turn is discussed further in reference to unfavorable spaces.

FLIP to pg. 39 for more info!

INTERRUPTING A TURN

A quick interjection into another player's turn is called an interrupt. Designers can integrate an interrupt into any component, allowing players to take action outside of their turn. For example:

+ A player may play a card that instantly counters an opponent's action.

+ A player may use tokens that can suddenly boost a game piece's speed.

+ An interrupt could also be a character's unique skill.

Some interrupts may be helpful, but more often, they hinder another player in some way. Interrupts are discussed further in reference to card play.

FLIP to pg. 94 for more info!

ELIMINATING A PLAYER

Some games include the possibility of player elimination. In this mechanic, players are eliminated from the game permanently, maybe as a result of poor performance, or else because an opponent has targeted them.

Although it adds an element of excitement, eliminating players too early from the game can be very unsatisfying. Sitting on the sidelines watching the rest of the competition is not pleasant.

To keep ejected players engaged, give them ways to interact with opponents, or even make their way back into the game. Sometimes players who have been eliminated can still win, for example, if they manage to retain a higher score than everyone else by the game's end.

Other times, players cannot keep their assets once they're eliminated; the assets could return to a communal pot, or the eliminated player could decide who gets them.

ACTIONS

 An action is anything you do in the game, by choice or by chance, during your turn or not. And sometimes in gaming, you take a chance with your choice.

When gaming offers you choices, every decision you make creates a unique ripple effect. But chance isn't always entirely eliminated from the equation. For example, if you decide to move your game piece from a list of options, the number of spaces you move may depend on a die roll. If you decide to draw a card, the deck gives you a random result.

These actions involve randomization, which means you're taking a chance with your choice. This balance between decision and luck is what establishes a fun and fair game.

ACTION POINTS

To give players multiple choices per turn, designers may offer them a limited amount of action points. These represent a unique type of currency to pay for the cost of an action. Usually players receive action points at the beginning of each round and can spend them on different tasks throughout their turn. They may be represented as cardboard cutout components or kept track of as a number in your head or on paper.

CLASSIC GAMING EXAMPLE
Checkers

Also known as Draughts, Checkers is an old-school wargame similar to Chess, in that the main goal is to capture or disable all of the opposing game pieces. The game pieces, called men or pawns, are allowed very few options, and only in certain situations.

Players can perform one action per turn with their chosen pawn. If the pawn has an open pathway, it can only move forward, diagonally on the checkered board, one space at a time. But if the circumstances are right, a pawn can jump over an opposing pawn and capture it.

If a pawn reaches the opposite end of the board, the pawn upgrades to a king (in some countries known as a queen). It is crowned with another game piece and granted greater mobility.

CHECKERED PAST

In traditional rules, a player may be penalized for not jumping a game piece when they could have. At the start of their turn, an opponent may seize the player's game piece that failed to jump and capture during the last turn.

Basically, it's a double punishment because not only did that player miss an opportunity, but they also now lose a game piece.

This practice is known as huffing, because players would customarily celebrate this bonus action by picking up the captured pawn and blowing on it.

If a pawn reaches the opposite end of the board, it upgrades to a king. It is crowned with another game piece.

FOLLOW

Some games use a follow mechanic, which triggers players to imitate what others have done. Sometimes this is a free action that players must perform; other times there is an associated cost to do so.

For example, one player may choose a specific action that then allows all other players to perform that same action immediately, out of turn. This could be as simple as one player drawing a card: In some games, their opponents can draw a card without cost, while in other games, they may have to discard a card first.

Sometimes the person who first performed the action gets a bonus if others follow. For example, if a player builds a road and others wanted to follow, that player could receive a bonus resource from the bank for each opponent who takes advantage of the follow action.

The follow mechanic keeps players on their toes, because they are always seeking opportunities to act outside of their regular turn. Be aware, though, that it can also slow down gameplay and make it hard to remember who is currently the active player. In this situation, tokens can be helpful to keep track of turn order.

RESTRICTIONS

While some mechanics increase the number of actions players can carry out, many games look for clever ways to restrict players. This means that players are restrained from doing particular things—not that they can never do them, just that they can do them only at certain times or under certain conditions. These restrictions can play out in many ways.

Command Cards

Any game that uses a deck of cards limits you to what you can draw or play from your hand. What's unique about command cards is that they limit you further by indicating specific locations or types of components. If a card indicates a specific area, then the card can only affect components in (or in relation to) that area. Equally, if a card indicates a specific component, then the card can only affect those components.

Command cards can show locations by depicting portions of the board itself or by using arrows to indicate specific areas. Different components are often indicated by a label, symbol, or shape.

For example, players may have units with circles, stars, or crescent moons depicted on them. When a card is played with a star on it, only the units with stars have the option of taking action, and all other units are restricted.

Often, the cards indicate how many components can take action. Many command cards also limit players by instructing which actions they can take such as moving or attacking.

A rondel can restrict players' actions.

Rondel

A curious way to restrict a player's action selection is to use a rondel, a small, flat disk that shows what actions are allowed each turn. Players set markers on different wedge-shaped spaces that indicate actions. Each turn, players may (or must, depending on the game) move their markers around the rondel. Where their marker lands shows which action they can perform that turn, either freely or through some cost. If the player wanted to choose a different option, then they would have to pay to move their marker to a different space on the rondel.

Like everything in gaming, there are many variations to rondels. Some games allow players to move around the rondel multiple spaces per turn for free. They can also be used for more than actions, such as what resource is currently available to you.

Action Drafting

Other action restrictions give an advantage to the player who goes first in the turn order and thus set limitations on those who go later in the round. This type is called action drafting, which provides one set of actions for all players, and you cannot pick the same action as someone else in the same round.

Players take turns choosing from a shared list of actions until each player has chosen one. Then, the list refreshes at the beginning of the next round. This can become problematic if the same person is going first every turn: They'll always have first choice. An alternating turn order is often used to solve this problem, swapping who goes first each round. In addition, designers can offer the opportunity to restore the list of actions before it runs out, in exchange for currency or resources.

Continues on Next Page ▶

Drafting

In general, drafting can apply to the selection of cards, resources, or any other aspect. It's a process where players choose one option per turn from a shared pool until all of the options have run dry. Drafting is discussed further in reference to cards.

FLIP to pg. 66 for more info!

A popular type of action drafting is worker placement, where players physically place a game piece on a designated space to represent an action. This helps evoke the theme of the game. Workers, for example, might perform separate tasks on a farm, such as gathering crops or building a fence to ward away threats. Worker placement means that the number of workers players control limits how many actions they can take. In some situations, players can earn new workers through their actions or at specific points in the game. On the other hand, players could lose workers if they get older or are sacrificed.

Some designers include different types of workers who can accomplish specific tasks. For example, there may be workers who can only build, collect resources, or transport materials or goods. Each type is unable to perform any other task. Some specialized workers can even create new locations. This advancement allows for new worker actions, location-based actions, and bonuses. Often, games provide ways of altering the worker's profession, at a cost, so that they can complete different tasks if needed.

Expanding the game even further, you can use dice as workers. This mechanic uses a die to represent each worker component. Each number of pips may represent a different worker type, a worker's attack strength, or how many resources a worker can acquire in one round.

A popular game-ending mechanic often used in worker placement games is a fixed number of rounds, which means that the game ends after a predetermined number of rounds have passed. This setup can simulate the passing of time or seasons.

Worker placement is discussed further in reference to *Intergalactic Laboratory*.

FLIP to pg. 119 for more info!

Strong Theme, Strong Game

Playing a game is often about experiencing a real-life activity through a metaphor, whether it be war, animal behavior patterns, cooking a meal, or forest fire prevention. For example, the game Hibernation applies a bear theme to all of the actions, resources, and other game parts. Even the currency is called "energy," and players must rest or "power nap" to obtain more.

Many people play games to enjoy a conceptual experience. If you are taking this route of design, be sure that a theme is evident and shines through the gameplay.

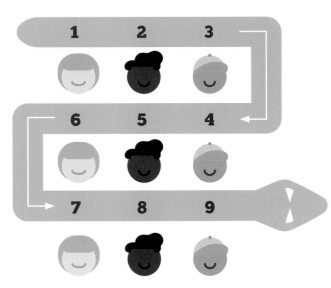

One type of turn order that works well with a draft is known as the serpentine method.

Tactics and Turn Order

A competitive tactic that players can use is called counter drafting. It means predicting the option an opponent may want and choosing it before they have the opportunity to do so. This course of action is taken purely to block an opponent from choosing it, even if it's not necessarily the option that would best suit your gameplay.

Generally, it's wise to use an alternating turn order when instituting any kind of drafting; otherwise, the player who selects first will always be at an advantage.

Previous sections have discussed turn order, but one type that works especially well with a draft is known as the boustrophedonic (boo-STREH-fee-DAW-nik), or serpentine, method. The process flows the way a farmer plows a field (or a homeowner mows the lawn), plowing one way and then turning and plowing the next row in the opposite direction, wasting no movement. The word *boustrophedon* translates from ancient Greek as "ox-turning."

Continues on Next Page ▶

Gaming Philosophy

It's important to know your opponent. Focus on your awareness. Imagine how your opponents are planning to win and what tactics they may use. But don't lose sight of your own plans.

Try to sense how you can counter your opponent while maintaining a clear vision of your own victory, playing efficiently and productively.

A turn order that is usually integrated into action drafting and worker placement is a claim turn order, which gives players control over the drafting. Players take turns choosing actions or placing workers according to a fixed turn order. The difference is, if they reach a point where it seems best for them to go first in the next round, then they could use their next action to claim the first player position. Players might choose to spend their action this way because they want priority to choose better options in the next round.

This turn order lends itself well to action drafting and worker placement because a player must choose to sacrifice something important, like an action or a worker, to alter the turn structure and claim going first. Traditionally, when altering turn order through a new claim, people then play in a clockwise direction from who made the claim.

Claim turn order can be problematic for designers to work into games, but it's potentially very interesting and can feel thematically on point. The power of control is integrated into a player's turn—it's not a separate precursor phase. Plus, players can't merely outspend each other, as in bid turn order.

Here's the problem. If it's not worth giving up an action to claim going first, whoever went first previously can retain that position, at no extra cost. One way to resolve this is to offer an incentive to those who do decide to claim the first position next round.

Passed Action Token

Another way of restricting action is to use a passed action token. For this mechanism, players can act only if they're holding an action token, which pays for the action. Once used, the token passes clockwise to the next player. This method works only if there are multiple action tokens in play, allowing players to act simultaneously; otherwise it's merely a fixed turn order. Passed action tokens are discussed further in reference to *Hovels & Hydras*.

FLIP to pg. 126 for more info!

Actions in Real Time

Some games stray from the typical pattern and manipulate *when* you can use actions. To do this, designers may use an action timer, as in Kitchen Rush and Space Dealers.

Typically, this mechanic employs a sand timer that players must apply to their actions, basically setting the game in real time. The difference is that instead of all players heeding a single timer, each player's actions have individual timers.

This mechanism forces players to play extra efficiently or face falling behind. Real time is discussed further in reference to turn order.

FLIP to pg. 26 for more info!

MONUMENTAL ACTIONS

Some mechanics allow players to perform monumental actions. They could be distinctive to each individual character, or they could be available to every player, at a cost or in a particular scenario.

Some of these powers are known as once-per-game abilities, because they are so great that they can turn the tides of battle. Usually, these are bonus actions that each player receives at the beginning of the game, and once players use them, they're gone. Sometimes, if players don't use them during the game, they're rewarded with extra points at the end.

An advantage token is a variation of a once-per-game ability. It also allows players to perform colossal acts, but instead of each player having this opportunity, only one player at a time does, per token. Once a player commits the monumental action, they must pass the token to another player according to the rules.

An example of such a powerful action may be that a player throws a lightning strike. If this is a once-per-game ability, the lightning strike could destroy a building, severely hampering the targeted opponent's ability to collect resources. If this is in the form of an advantage token, the effect could be that the targeted opponent(s) must discard a set of resources, a less severe repercussion.

Either way, this would provide an excellent opportunity for the player who used the action to catch up.

A player throws a lightning strike, creating an opportunity to catch up.

MOVEMENT

The process of navigating a game piece, or any component, is known as movement, a fundamental mechanic in gaming. It means that you are shifting a component across one or more spaces to a different part of the board. Moving a component is a specific type of action that allows players to accomplish their goals.

Some games provide movement points, which pay for movement. A set of these points may be given to players to distribute among their components as needed. Sometimes, particular spaces may cost more movement points because they are challenging terrain for your figurines to pass across, like a mountain or swamp.

Similarly, players could instead use currency or a resource to move. Requiring players to spend points, currency, or resources drives them to strategize their movement instead of leaving it up to randomization.

CLASSIC GAMING EXAMPLE
Parcheesi

There are many ways to assist trailing players or inhibit leaders in order to keep gameplay balanced. In Parcheesi, an ancient Indian game originally known as Pachisi, players must roll the exact number needed (on one die, or the total of both) to land on the final center space. If a player moves all of their game pieces into the center space, they win the game. As a result, the leading player will probably spend multiple turns rolling the dice, trying to get their last game piece into the final space.

This allows players in the back to continue moving in hopes of catching the leader. Die rolls are unpredictable, however, and players in the front may rapidly reach the finish line.

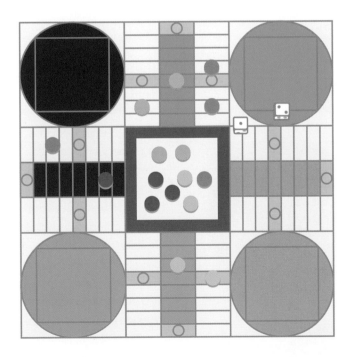

Players must roll the exact number needed to land on the final center space.

RACES

A race is a common game-ending and winning mechanism. The goal, of course, is to get your game piece to the finish line first. Often, players use a component of randomization, such as a die or a spinner, to determine their movement (roll-and-move or spin-and-move). Another type of race game is one that ends when the leading player reaches a particular number of points, rather than a finish line.

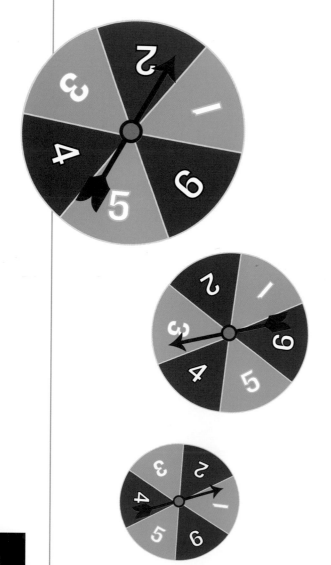

Catch the Leader

While the idea of a racing game may seem simple, there are many ways to make it exciting. You could use a catch the leader mechanism: Players get advantages or disadvantages based on their position in the race.

For example, players who are falling behind are given more dice to throw than the player who is currently in the lead. The first-place player could receive only one die, while second and third place could get two dice each, and fourth place, three dice. The extra dice could allow the player in last place to slingshot forward because they have better odds of rolling a higher number.

The order of players' components can be of great importance. As well as affecting the dice, the order may influence scoring, bonuses, or turn order.

Different Dice

Another way to spice up a classic race would be to utilize different dice movement. For example, the dice could represent the multiple gears of a bike or a car. The lowest speed could be represented by a small numbered die, like a four-sided die (d4). The speeds could increase with each successive gear to a higher numbered die, like the conventional six-sided die (d6), then up to an eight-sided (d8), then 10-sided (d10) and 12-sided (d12). You could even accelerate all the way up to a 20-sided die (d20). Or the speeds could increase from one d6 up to five d6.

The point is that the higher you shift the gear (and the higher the possible outcome), the greater the capacity for speed (and the broader the range of the die rolls).

Favorable and Unfavorable Spaces

A race could also be more intriguing with spaces on the board that are favorable or unfavorable, propelling you in a different direction or holding you back. This momentum or restriction could be caused by something natural, such as a strong breeze or a flowing river, or something mechanical, like a conveyer belt.

How a favorable space works is up to you, but an easy approach would be to add bonus value to your current movement. For example, a board with a race track could have spaces that act like boost pads, projecting game pieces forward. In this case, the boost pads could allow game pieces to move an extra space or two.

A game board could also have unfavorable spaces that would hold players back, such as challenging terrain like high grass or rocky paths. These spaces could subtract from your die roll, decreasing your movement. Generally, unfavorable spaces affect players even when they're simply passing through. Landing on an unfavorable space could cause a player to lose their next turn. Losing a turn is discussed further in reference to turn order.

FLIP to pg. 27 for more info!

Player Elimination

Sometimes, race games result in player elimination. A game may be about racing as well as surviving an oncoming threat. Whoever is trailing at the end of each round could take damage, eventually being eliminated.

For example, players may take on the roles of rebel ships fleeing a massive tyrannical government ship. Whichever rebel ship is in last place at the end of the round would take damage from an oncoming attack; over time, the damage would destroy them. Player elimination is discussed further in reference to hidden roles and deduction.

FLIP to pg. 74 for more info!

MOVING IN STRANGE AND UNUSUAL WAYS

Movement can occur in many unique ways. Mancala, from an Arabic word meaning "to move," is a perfect example. This mechanic (and family of games) focuses on movement and skill, grounded in counting and calculations—with no element of chance whatsoever.

In mancala-based games, players take all the game pieces from one space and place them one by one in each successive space. The number of spaces you travel is determined by how many game pieces are in the starting location. The last place a game piece lands holds special importance, which varies depending on the game. The ultimate goal of mancala-based games is to capture the majority of the neutral game pieces that players share.

Another way to interpret the mancala mechanic is to view the neutral pieces as movement points. When you gather them up, you can move as many spaces as pieces you have, as long as you are dropping one off at each successive space. This initial action is free, once per turn, though there are versions of mancala that allow for players to strategically earn many more moves each turn.

Another unusual form of movement is when game pieces are confined to a unique movement pattern, as in Chess. When moving this way, game pieces can only shift based on particular arrangements. For example, the knight piece, usually represented by a horse, moves two squares straight then one square perpendicular.

The potential movements and actions of any given component are called its force projection. It's the limited set of choices that each component has available to make; what they are capable of. Force projection is literally the power that a game piece projects, the distance and degree to which it can exert power. Some game pieces can push opponents, capture them, or even send them back to their starting position, as in Sorry!.

As with the knight from Chess, it's important to be aware of a piece's potential movement, where it could end up, and what damage it could cause. Assess the force projection of your opponent's components (all that they may do on their turn) so that you can make wise decisions based on that power. Force projection is discussed further in reference to *Hovels & Hydras*.

FLIP to pg. 127 for more info!

Ancient Gaming

Mancala-style game boards are ancient: Their discovery in the Sahara Desert dates back to about 3000 BCE, when the land was a fertile plain. Some scholars debate whether these stone boards were an early abacus or counting aid. But mancala-based games are so simple—playable with beans and holes in the dirt—that it's easy to imagine the games are even older.

Measured Movement

Certain types of games use maps, miniatures, and measurement, which demands extreme precision: Players use rulers to determine where components can move.

With measurement, the map does not require a grid or spaces. The miniatures, or figurines, have predetermined stats, based on standard ruler measurements, that dictate their movement.

For example, one figurine may be able to move 5 inches (12 cm); to move, the player must measure out 5 inches from the game piece toward the destination. If there is challenging terrain to cross, or an elevation change, the measurement is reduced to show that it's harder to trek these areas.

As a designer, you can use a grid on your map instead of making players measure. Players may then only move square by square, but many find this approach simpler.

If measurement- or grid-based games include combat, the miniatures must have a proper line of sight to attack opponents. Players can check the line of sight by lining up a string from a miniature to its target. If no objects or props obstruct the twine, then the line of sight is true and clear for an attack. Traditionally, if even a minor corner of blockage is in the way, then the line is obstructed. Line of sight is discussed further in reference to *Hovels & Hydras*.

FLIP to pg. 127 for more info!

In some games, using a string, a ruler, or a grid is replaced with a game board that uses color-coded regions. The colored spaces on the board show what your miniature can see, based on where it's standing.

For example, if your game takes place in a house, the hallway may use purple spaces and the library off the hallway may use green spaces. This color coordination tells players who they can target with attacks. A player on a green space (in the library) can only target other players on green spaces (also in the library). They cannot target a player on a purple space (in the hallway). If they are standing in the doorway of the room, then that space may be multicolored, indicating that the player can see both what is in the library and in the hallway.

There's an intuitive understanding at play because of how rooms and houses work in the real world. One cannot attack through walls, and proper line of sight is established when two people are standing in the same room or one is standing in the doorway. Games with colored spaces do not require measurement; miniatures can instead use movement points or any other mechanic needed to move spaces.

Miniatures must have a proper line of sight to attack opponents.

BOARDS & MAPS

Boards and maps display locations and denote spaces where you can place game pieces, cards, or other components. Though boards and maps are similar, maps are sometimes used as a prop; the map is used for reference as opposed to a place for physically placing components.

Maps typically use grids while boards traditionally have customized spaces for traveling. A gridded map is covered evenly with either hexagons or squares. Of course, there are plenty of game boards with grids on them that aren't a map; Checkers and Chess are excellent examples.

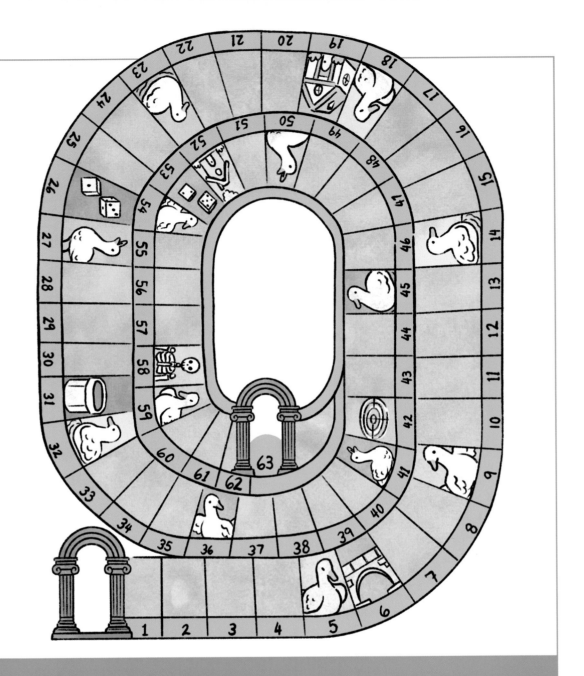

The Royal Game of Goose

Modern thematic board games trace back to the Royal Game of Goose, created in Italy in the late 1500s. It introduced illustrative elements and conceptual gameplay at a time when games were primarily mathematical and metaphorical. It is similar to Snakes & Ladders in that it relies entirely upon chance, making it virtually a lottery.

The board was originally an inward spiral with 63 spaces, and once the game took off to other countries, variations quickly occurred. This thematic game follows the actions of a goose. Locations on the board include the Bridge, the Maze, and the Spring (or Well), which causes a player to lose two consecutive turns because they are busy bathing in it.

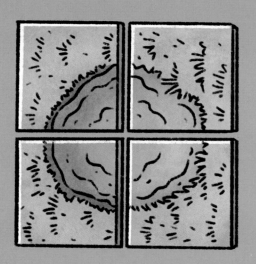 

Combining square tiles can result in completing a feature.

MODULAR MAPS AND TILE LAYING

A fascinating variation on generic game board design is the use of modular boards, multiple maps, or other components, combining various parts to create a whole. It's common to use cards or tiles to build a board, or even full game boards to add onto or swap with the original board. These variations could represent new areas that have been found or old areas that have somehow changed.

For example, players may be able to explore a mummy's tomb represented by a large board. Somewhere on the board, there's a locked gate, and if they find the right artifacts to open that gate, then the tomb is expanded with a new board or set of tiles. This format is considered constrained because players understand that there are limits to the exploration.

In contrast, many games are driven by world building and use an unconstrained style. The format of map addition allows players to venture off in any direction they please, limited only by their playing surface and components.

Building an unconstrained map during gameplay works well with the mechanism of tile laying. Tiles may be hexagonal, square, or rectangular, and are often acquired randomly from a central pile. Tile-laying can result in consistently unique gaming sessions because the map expands differently each time you play.

Dominoes must match up precisely at the edges.

In many variations, the connections made between the tiles must match up precisely at the edges. For example, in Dominoes, when a new domino is laid down, it must touch a domino with a matching value. In many tile-laying games, combining tiles results in a feature completion.

When players complete a feature, it means that the tiles have been connected into a recognizable composition. The features could represent anything, such as a fenced-in grassy enclosure, a lake, or an entire kingdom. Such connections are discussed further in reference to ownership and control.

FLIP to pg. 58 for more info!

Some modular boards allow movement in three dimensions: not only left, right, forward and back, but also up and down. Allowing three-dimensional movement opens the door to a vast array of options and strategy. As opposed to using modular boards to display three dimensions, designers may also use tokens or props to indicate height or depth.

Be aware, though, that gameplay can become confusing because of the vastness of space.

You can make the use of multiple maps even more interesting by including a mini-map. The mini-map acts as a zoomed-in version of the larger one, where gamers can play out scaled-down conflicts in greater focus, while the larger board displays more information.

Continues on Next Page ▶

Boards & Maps

Manipulating Maps

We've discussed many ways that a map can expand; alternatively, some games use the exact opposite method, reducing the board during gameplay. This shrinking is known as map reduction and can happen in several ways. Perhaps large chunks of the board are drifting away because you are playing as penguins, voyaging on floating platforms of ice. Or maybe the tiles that your game piece steps on disappear at the end of each turn, because they're platforms sinking into molten lava from the pressure of your footsteps.

It could be up to the players to choose which tiles to remove, or it could be because of another mechanic. The reduction of a map can also be much less dramatic. It may be that it only occurs once per game because of a specific accomplishment or mistake.

Another way of manipulating the board is known as map deformation. This mechanism plays out in many ways. Some games rotate or shift part of the game board, while others manipulate the entire board itself. Any tiles that move take components along with them.

Some distortions block off large portions of the board for a length of time. Alterations could also occur at the end of each round to represent time passing, like the shifting of seasons that provides unique resources. Alternatively, distortions could be a result of player interaction, like pulling a switch to set off a shifting of tiles. Map deformation alters gameplay, making it a primary mechanic when used in any game.

SPECIAL LOCATIONS

Instead of manipulating the map itself, you could manipulate how game pieces can move across it. One such way would be to offer shortcuts, which give players a way to travel quickly across the board by landing on a specific location. Or movement can happen as if through a portal: The instant your game piece steps on the space, it's warped across the entire map. Or perhaps it's simply an alternative path that, if landed on, allows you to skip ahead, in fewer moves than usual, by avoiding spaces.

As a way of upping the ante, designers could require a cost to use the shortcuts. Shortcuts are discussed further in reference to *Rain Toads.*

A format that rewards players each turn that they remain in a particular location on the board is known as king of the hill. Traditionally this mechanic is viewed as a single person maintaining a position of power, but in many games, this position can be shared by multiple players. The longer a player can stay at the top, the more they'll be rewarded (with resources, currency, or other bonuses), increasing their chances of winning.

FLIP to pg. 116 for more info!

Map reduction occurs as chunks of the board drift away in this South Pole-themed game.

CLASSIC GAMING EXAMPLE
Snakes & Ladders

An excellent example of a game that includes shortcuts, a simple fixed turn order, and one primary action is Snakes & Ladders. It originated in India before the eighteenth century, where it was initially known as Snake Dice. The size of the board and its grid varies from version to version, but the core rules have stayed the same. Its simplicity is what makes the game so timeless.

Players roll a die on their turn and move the resulting number of spaces. Many spaces have shortcuts, and what's interesting is that not all the shortcuts are positive. Strictly by chance, players may be eaten by snakes or rise rapidly through the grid, leaving the game utterly void of choice. There is no real way of improving from game to game.

A DATE WITH DESTINY

The theme of Snakes & Ladders is based on karma or destiny. Because of the lack of choice, it's easy for very young players to grasp. The only option you do have is how you choose to react to the positive and negative outcomes.

Good sportsmanship is a powerful way to manage your emotions. You may be excited from performing well or upset from failures, but you can still find balance in your actions to keep your ego and sensitivity in check. Discover pride in doing your best and realize there is always another opportunity to try again.

Strictly by chance, players may be eaten by snakes or rise rapidly through the grid.
Choice is completely absent.

RANDOMIZATION

 One of the most used and well-known ways of generating randomization, an unpredictable result, is by rolling a die. Dice themselves have been used for ages: 20-sided dice made of serpentinite were discovered in Egypt, dating back to about the third century BCE.

Early dice were quite uneven in shape, meaning that some ancient games of chance also included quite a bit of skill to achieve the desired toss. To many, this felt like cheating.

In ancient Rome, they took extra precautions to ensure fairness by instituting a device called a dice tower, dating back to the fourth century CE, which is still used in gaming today. These structures were initially made of bone and stood about 7.5 inches (20 cm) tall, inscribed with elaborate designs.

Enclosed within the structure is a series of ramps. Players drop dice into the top of the tower so they can tumble down the ramps and fall out of the bottom, randomized.

Today, dice towers are built from just about anything (though most likely not bone!) and come in many designs.

Dice rolling is prevalent in gaming, and even the basis for entire games, like Yahtzee (originally Yacht), where players roll multiple dice hoping to acquire particular combinations. It's known as a Roll-and-Write game, because players throw dice and record the results. Sometimes, only a basic score is kept, but other times there are more complicated puzzles or calculations to complete. This mechanism can also be used with a deck of cards, known appropriately as Flip-and-Write.

Superstition & Luck Particles

Many players hold superstition in high regard when throwing dice, and indeed, we may all find ourselves wishing for a momentary act of magic when rolling. What could be more fitting surrounding an object based on luck? Many superstitious players swap out dice if they seem to roll low numbers continuously or place dice with the desired results facing up before rolling, allowing any luck particles to settle and influence their outcome. They may even go as far as forbidding other players from touching their dice, insisting that each player must have their own.

PLAYING WITH OUTCOMES

Roll-and-write games often provide ways to adjust the odds so that the desired result is achieved more easily. One way is to use a dice selection mechanism. Players roll multiple dice but don't include every die in the outcome. Sometimes players can select the result, while other times there is a rule in place to determine the outcome.

One example of dice selection could be that players are given three six-sided dice (d6) to roll and choose only two of the resulting values. A contrasting example could be that players are given three 10-sided dice (d10) and the rules state that they must use the middle-value roll. Dice selection is discussed further in reference to *Rain Toads*.

FLIP to pg. 117 for more info!

A pair of mechanisms that put greater control into the player's hands are known as locking and re-rolling. These mechanics allow you to keep good throws and re-roll dice for a better possible outcome. For example, you have a set of three d6 to roll, and you are looking for the highest possible result. If the outcomes are 1, 2, and 5, then you might lock the die that rolled a 5 and re-roll the rest, hoping for higher values. Depending on the game, you may be able to lock any number of dice and re-roll multiple times.

You don't have to use a die to achieve randomization. You could also use a spinner, pieces of paper mixed up and pulled out of a hat, or a deck of cards.

Other general forms of adjusting random outcomes are known broadly as probability management. Just as the name indicates, players manipulate the likelihood of getting the result they desire. Instead of locking in great rolls, players alter their current throw by using tokens that change the outcome. Probability management is discussed further in reference to cards and deck construction.

FLIP to pg. 63 for more info!

Continues on Next Page ▶

Dice Across Space & Time

Researchers have discovered similarities in dice and games found among vastly different ancient civilizations. For example, the Aztec game of Patolli and the Indian game of Pachisi shared many similar features. In both, game pieces move along boards that are cross-like in shape, and players determine this movement by throwing binary lots, which are like two-sided dice.

The Aztec game of Patolli used five black beans with white dots on one side, while the Indian game of Pachisi used six cowrie shells for lots. Cowrie shells are naturally distinctly different on each side.

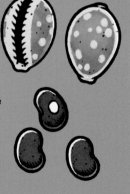

Other remarkable materials used to create lots were bone, brass, fruit pits, ivory, leather, limestone, nuts, pottery, and wood. It's believed that lots originated with soothsayers and oracles who used them for mystical readings.

Critical Hits and Failures

An interesting way to alter generic outcomes without player intervention would be to use a critical hits and failures mechanism. Players roll a die, or multiple dice, and particular outcomes are considered extremely good or excessively awful. Usually, it's the highest and lowest values that provide these intensive hits and failures, respectively. In a generic roll-and-move race game, you could apply a critical failure anytime a player rolls a 1 on a six-sided die (d6), causing them to move backward a space instead of forward.

Typically, critical hits and failures coincide with stat check resolution. With this mechanism, players throw dice intending to match or exceed a predetermined number so they can accomplish a particular task. The task may involve a skill, such as picking a lock, or it may involve a passive defense, such as resisting poison. If the result is critical, then what would've happened on a regular success or failure is amplified.

The difficulty factor is indicated by which type of dice are used and how many. In general, the higher the predetermined number, the more difficult the task is to accomplish. Stat check resolution is discussed further in reference to adventure role playing games.

FLIP to pg. 80 for more info!

The results of critical hits and failures can vary in complexity when applied. If applied when rolling for movement, then a player may earn an extra space with a successful critical hit. But the scenario would be very different if applied to stat check resolution: For example, a player is attempting to attack an opponent with their bow and arrow but rolls a critical failure. In that case, a complex outcome could be that not only did the player miss the attack, but their bowstring also snapped and is now useless.

A player is attempting to attack an opponent with their bow and arrow but rolls a critical failure.

It's important to note that critical hits and failures require a maximum and minimum number to be established ahead of time.

Risk and Reward

Similar to the concept of great successes and terrible disasters through critical hits and failures is a risk-and-reward mechanism. It's a gamble: You hope to achieve something great as you risk something terrible. Your reward may be a way of taking down the leader or moving you to the front of the pack. But be careful, because the poor result could instead plunge you into a far worse position.

If you are using cards, an easy way to use this mechanic could be that half the cards in the deck send you forward one space, while the other half send you backward. Risk-and-reward is discussed further in reference to *Hovels & Hydras*.

FLIP to pg. 126 for more info!

CLASSIC GAMING EXAMPLE
Backgammon

Some games employ unique methods of managing probability, and Backgammon is an example. Its rules allow players to set their pawns, also known as blots, onto unique spaces that raise their chances of getting a good roll (or lower their opponent's). Probability management could be utilized creatively in your own game. Perhaps for each card you reveal from your hand, you get to add 1 to your next die roll.

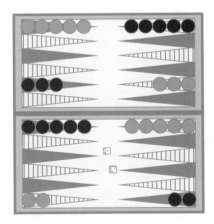

In Backgammon, pawns are known as blots.

CURRENCY & OWNERSHIP

Currency goes by many names, including coin, money, and cash. Players earn and use currency, as well as points and resources, in countless ways. They are interchangeable assets that can help to keep gameplay balanced.

Depending on the game, a set of currency can purchase resources that can be sold back for cash. Some games use money or resources to equal victory points (points that count toward winning the game) or vice versa. Since players can use currency, resources, and victory points in corresponding ways, that means that they are basically interchangeable.

Secret resources can be hidden behind a view blocker.

SPENDING AND DEFENDING ASSETS

It's important to note that when exchanging these assets for one another, they may be worth differing values. For example, a game may provide an opportunity to use four resources to purchase one victory point. The victory point is worth more because it allows you to win, while resources are more common. But in other games, resources might not be so common. It all depends on the game and an individual's circumstances.

When assets are always available, it means that they cannot be exhausted. But when assets are limited in quantity, you may want to obtain them before your opponents. As a designer, you can use the exhaustion mechanic to limit availability. The exhaustion of a particular asset or component could trigger an event or even the end of an entire game. This limitation could pertain to any asset; any component may be in limited supply. Exhaustion is discussed further in reference to cards.

FLIP to pg. 65 for more info!

In many games, the assets that you collect are exposed for all to see, while in other games, they are kept a secret. Occasionally a view blocker is provided, like a screen or multipaneled cardboard stand. This defense allows you to stow away hidden victory points, resources, and currency to keep opponents guessing at your hoard of assets.

To gain new assets in a game, often players must first have ownership over something, but in order to own something, they need assets to buy it. This problem is solved by providing ownership, assets, or both at the beginning of a game. These assets come from a bank that is part of the game. A bank is a place for holding currency or resources not actively in play, and sometimes it can offer opportunities for further interaction. Banks are expanded upon in reference to *Rain Toads*.

FLIP to pg. 116 for more info!

If you're not able to afford a purchase but believe it's a worthy buy, then you may be able to take out a loan from the bank. Taking a loan is a quick way to gain more assets, but you'll have to pay them back, and always with interest. It's a risk and requires strategy to manage.

INCOME

When players are able to earn assets through gameplay, it's called income. For example: A player is provided with currency at the beginning of a game. That player then lands on a space and uses the provided currency to purchase the space. Any time their opponent lands on that space, as the owner, that player earns income (in the form of currency from that opponent). Accumulating income through ownership is a common form of earning assets, as in Monopoly.

Income could be established by the result of a randomizer, such as the roll of a die at the beginning of each turn. Dice could inform players which areas on the board earn resources this turn, depending on whether players own components in that area, as in Catan. Or dice can simply tell players which resources to collect and how many. When players earn income in these ways, it's considered random production. You could use any component of randomization to generate assets; for example, cards could inform the players of what to gain.

Some games offer players upgrades, or improvements, to their purchases. Players may swap out their initial buy with an enhanced version. Players may exchange a small building for a larger one that doubles the asset growth. These alterations provide more resources, abilities, or features, increasing your in-game worth. Upgrades are discussed further in reference to leveling up.

FLIP to pg. 79 for more info!

In some situations, owned assets can grow on their own—a mechanism known as automatic resource growth. For example, keeping multiple animals fenced in together could produce an offspring each round. Usually, the new offspring is used in the same way as the resources that created it; it is not limited in its use because it is new. In the world of gaming, sometimes things like gender or age don't enter the equation, simplifying things. This collecting of new assets can be viewed as another form of income.

Automatically produce a new resource every round.

Mechanics

HARD WORK PAYS OFF

Sometimes discounts on purchases are available, if players fit the necessary circumstances. Discounts can make acquisitions affordable (especially if players would rather avoid a loan), although, sometimes discounts require that players spend money first on something else.

For example, if a player purchases a particular building, they might be offered an extreme price cut for a specific card or set of cards. This effect could stack up as the game progresses, making it easier to obtain more expensive purchases because of multiple discounts. A discount can also be offered through simpler means, such as setting your game piece on a particular space.

An interesting way to earn assets is through the use of a contract. A contract requires that resources be acquired or a task be accomplished in exchange for currency or points. As when a quarry miner sells stones for money, contracts often ask for cash in return for resources. It's a way of getting paid for collecting assets or accomplishing tasks. Contracts are often presented in the form of a card and can be distributed privately or made publicly available. Public contracts can cause tension between opponents, driving players to produce results as fast as possible.

A mechanism often used in conjunction with contracts is pick-up and deliver. To fulfill a contract, players must pick up an asset in one place and deliver it to another, in exchange for the reward.

Gambling or betting can produce quick assets, but it's always left to chance. You could win big or lose everything. To place a bet, you provide an asset for a chance at winning a larger pot of assets. It's a quick way to sidestep earning assets the old-fashioned way, but players always have a low chance at success.

Purchases result in ownership. In many games, the purpose is to achieve ownership over a collection that together is more valuable than simply the sum of its parts. A collection could represent a set of items, a series of houses and roads that establish a society, or a string of military posts.

Continues on Next Page ▶

Gambling in Gaming

When referring to gambling in gaming, it's essential to make some distinctions. All discussions in this book of betting currency refer to in-game money only.

It's true that any game could be played for actual cash, from Mancala to Chess, and that some games, like Poker, are inherently gambling focused. Betting real-world money has negative connotations, but this should not be held against games as a whole. The very idea of taking a risk is a healthy concept to understand and practice. There is risk in everything you do, but you can't let that prevent you from living.

A different type of gamble is known as push-your-luck or press-your-luck. Gambling in this way means that players can bet what they've already won in a wager for an even more fabulous prize— but could potentially lose everything. Fundamentally, if you never stop pressing your luck, then you always end up losing. Knowing when to walk away with a win instead of pushing too far is extremely important.

Collecting a group of connected components can help you block opponents or isolate them to an area of the board. In some games, there are ways of crossing an opponent's connected components, but at a cost; in other games, connections can't be broken. In general, connections can be viewed as the linking together of any given components. Connections are discussed further in reference to *Intergalactic Laboratory*.

FLIP to pg. 119 for more info!

Sometimes connections represent motion dynamically, like guiding a laser beam to its target. This subset of connections is known as chaining. It's a specialization that limits players to adding new game pieces to only the tip of the path or according to other restrictive rules. Chaining helps to conceptualize a component's movement without actually moving any game pieces.

CONNECTIONS AND ROUTE BUILDING

When a game asks players to create links between specific destinations, it's using a network-building, or route-building, subset of connections. Players fulfill network requirements by creating routes between destinations to collect a reward.

For example, you may be trying to get customers to use your train service, but to earn their ticket you have to establish routes to specific destinations. This access allows the customer to get to and from the places they require via their ticket. With network building, you can receive victory points for earning tickets and creating specific routes, as in Ticket to Ride. Game-ending and winning conditions can be dependent upon building specific connections.

In more straightforward route-building situations, players may be required to connect one specific end of a game board to another, which would win the game. These are often abstract games that use less complicated connections.

Another engaging way to use network building is to utilize line drawing, which means that players make their connections by physically drawing lines.

This differs from other network-building games that have boards with routes already printed on them. In both types of games, players must purchase, build, or somehow trigger connections to claim ownership, but in a line-drawing system, the board can be different every time you play because players are drawing it.

Truly, line drawing can be much more versatile. In some scenarios, each player has their own map, as in Cartographers, which plays more like a grid coverage game. Abstract games and grid coverage are discussed further in reference to puzzles.

FLIP to pg. 83 for more info!

CLASSIC GAMING EXAMPLE
Pigs in a Pen

A more traditional example of a line-drawing game would be Dots and Boxes, also known more humbly as Boxes, or more playfully as Pigs in a Pen. It's a remarkably accessible game. All you need to play is a writing utensil and a surface, making it a paper-and-pencil game, but you can use more modern tools, like a digital drawing application.

First, place dots into a grid of any size, though if the grid is smaller than 5×5, the path to victory is far too obvious. Then, two or more players take turns drawing lines to connect two adjacent dots that are unjoined vertically or horizontally, but not diagonally. Whoever creates a 1×1 box by completing the fourth line claims the box, earns one point, and goes again.

The game is over once every dot is joined, creating boxes and making the player with the most points the victor. Often, players will mark which boxes they control by writing their initials or coloring inside the box with a particular color.

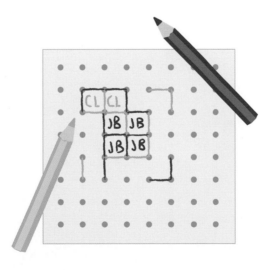

Whoever creates a 1×1 box by completing the fourth line claims the box, earns one point, and goes again.

AREA CONTROL

Purchases and ownership are forms of control. The ownership of assets and components is one type of control, but control over territory or space in a game, known as area control, can be equally important. Boards or maps can contain individual spaces, regions, and whole territories. Players who occupy the most regions, or an entire territory, can receive bonuses or advantages, such as special components, extra resources, or possibly dice rolls at an advantage.

How are locations occupied or controlled in a game? You may typically think of a building on a game board as an indicator of ownership or occupancy. In wargames, players use figurines referred to as troop types (soldiers, tanks, and other war machines) with their own unique stats and characteristics.

Some locations can have a limit to the number of components (resources, players, pieces) within it. Like a busy waterpark on a hot day, the location can accommodate only a certain amount.

The mechanism of area control allows a player to control a location or an entire territory. If opponents enter your space, you may attack them to defend it. If your defense fails, you may lose control, although control or ownership can exchange hands through negotiation as well. Negotiation is discussed further in reference to alliances.

FLIP to pg. 70 for more info!

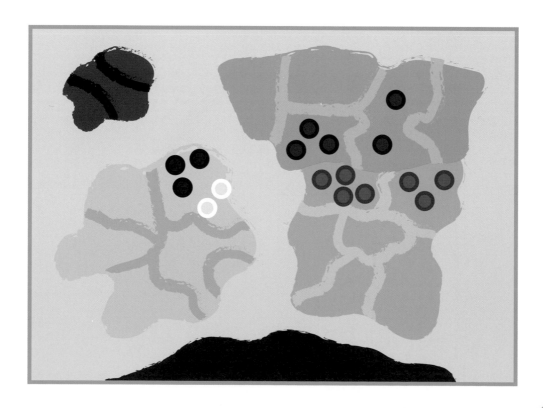

CLASSIC GAMING EXAMPLE
Go

Go is a spatial game of placement. Where you place your game pieces is important because they permanently occupy that position unless they are captured. Through the method of enclosure, players string their stones together to surround unoccupied areas and claim them or surround opponent's game pieces and capture them. Both ways earn victory points.

BALANCING YIN AND YANG

The ancient area control game of Go is one of the oldest board games in the world. Its origins in China date back to the early 2000s BCE, where it was first known as *Wei-qi* (way-chee), which roughly means "surrounding pieces."

This translation is apt because the purpose of the game is to enclose vacant areas, and surround your opponent, by occupying territory on a game board. Opposing players choose between black and white stones, which represent the yin and yang, an ancient concept that balances complementary opposing forces.

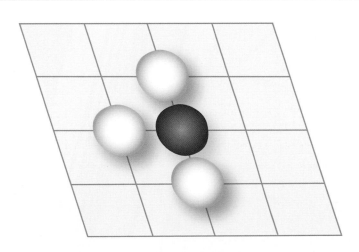

Using the method of enclosure, players string their stones together
to surround and capture the opponent's game pieces.

In some games, players improve their decks by purchasing new cards from a bank.

CARDS

A deck of cards is a staple in gaming, one that goes back centuries, with evidence that playing cards have existed since 900 CE.

Naysayers throughout history have identified cards as "the devil's picture book," believing that all card games focus on gambling. Some do, but many don't, and now we know that card games are a fun and challenging source of intellectual recreation.

Card games that involve hand comparison, like Poker and Blackjack, often begin with a betting phase. Players then reveal their hands and compare whose is best based on a standardized ranking system, and the winner collects the entire pool of bets.

Games of gambling like these rely on hidden information and bluffing. The players may act as though they are hiding something great in their hand of cards, when in reality, it may be dismal. It's all about staying in the game when others bow out.

Players can use anything to gamble with, such as gaming currency, victory points, or even food like candy or snacks. Betting is discussed further in reference to gambling.

FLIP to pg. 57 for more info!

Modern gaming employs a plethora of innovative card mechanics. A popular genre known as collectible card games (CCG) exemplifies many of the best-known mechanisms. Outside of actual gameplay, players build a deck of cards through purchase or trade, which is an important part of the game.

CCGs should not be confused with the deck-building mechanic, where card collection and deck construction do occur during gameplay. When deck-building, players try to improve their decks throughout the game by gathering new cards from a bank of cards available to all.

Acquiring cards in a deck-building format is considered a delayed purchase, because you aren't able to use them right away. Often, the newly purchased card, or cards, are either shuffled into your deck or placed in your discard pile, making them unavailable until the next draw or shuffling of your discard pile into your deck. Through this adjustment of their deck, players are using probability management to increase their odds of drawing what they desire. Probability management is discussed further in reference to randomization.

FLIP to pg. 51 for more info!

Tarot Cards

Lots, the ancestors of dice, were originally used for divination, while tarot cards were originally a game! Their occult functions date back to the late eighteenth century, while their roots in Italy as a competitive game go back more than 500 years earlier.

Today, tarot cards are designed for fortune-telling, gaming, and collecting, although almost any gaming deck can be used for fortune-telling, or vice versa. In Europe, Tarot is still a commonly played card game.

COMMON MECHANISMS

A breakdown of operations for a card game could begin with drawing a card. Many games provide a card at the start of each turn; others require that you use an action point, then add that card to your hand or put it directly into play. Using a card draw mechanic simply means that you take a card from the top of the deck.

If you have a hand of cards, then you're using hand management. You hold some cards while choosing to play others as efficiently and optimally as possible. Playing a card could cost you resources, or be completely free because each player gets to play one free card per turn.

Many games limit the number of cards you hold in your hand. This restriction makes it challenging to keep cards for long, especially if you're unable to use them due to high cost or lack of opportunity. There can be limits on deck size, cards in your hand, and any other component.

As players design their decks, they're adjusting the chances of receiving specific cards, focusing on the tactics that work. Once the deck reaches exhaustion, and cards can no longer be drawn a reaction may follow, like shuffling the discard pile to become the new deck or losing the game outright. This process is not limited to cards; it can also apply to other components, like ending the game after exhausting resources. Exhaustion is discussed further in reference to currency, resources, and points.

FLIP to pg. 55 for more info!

Thwart Expectations . . . or Not

Once gamers get used to a rule, subverting their expectations can make for exciting game crafting. As a designer, you could have nothing happen after a deck is exhausted, leaving it up to the players to choose when and how to bring the deck back into play.

The mechanics laid out in this book intend to energize your mind with ideas, but try not to get stuck on the examples. Be creative in your game design. At the same time, don't feel pressured to design some new mechanism.

DRAFTING

A common practice with collectible card games is drafting from sealed booster packs. This is an exciting format—it's impossible to know what's in each package before they're opened, although players are usually aware of the cards they might obtain due to marketing hype, as with Magic: the Gathering.

One way to draft with sealed packs is called a parallel pick-and-pass process. This means that each player has their own package of cards that they are opening and looking through. They pick one to keep and then pass the pack to the next player clockwise. At the same time, each player receives a stack of cards from the player to their immediate right, who also picked one and passed. This process continues until each stack has been exhausted.

Important note: The number of cards per pack needs to be equal to or greater than the number of players if you want each stack to make it around to each person at least once. Often the purpose of the draft is to create a deck using only the cards you've drafted. Therefore, the process usually needs to occur multiple times for players to have enough cards. When opening multiple packs, it's helpful to alternate the passing order after each round to keep things fair.

It is not required that players have unsealed booster packs to use this mechanism. A game could simply distribute stacks of cards to each player, as in 7 Wonders. This mechanism can also be used with only one stack of cards, as opposed to each player getting their own; this is referred to plainly as pick-and-pass. The active player acquires a set of cards, picks one, and then passes them around for each player to choose one, like in Lords of Waterdeep.

Then there is the vastly different Rochester draft. Every card to be drafted is laid out, visible for all to see. There's no hidden information. Players take turns choosing one card at a time until they're all gone. Those who pay attention will observe the cards their opponents are choosing. Note: This draft can cause player paralysis at the magnitude of options, thinking through all potential strategies before picking a card.

Drafts usually conclude when every card has been chosen but may end because a timer has gone off or all players have passed their turn. Drafting is discussed further in reference to action drafting.

FLIP to pg. 31 for more info!

Player 1 starts with a stack of four cards.
Each player chooses a card from the stack until it is exhausted.

| Player 1 selects one card of the four. | → | The remaining cards are passed to Player 2. | → | Player 2 selects one card of the remaining. |

SPLAYING AND MELDING

The card mechanisms of splaying and melding appear in a multitude of classic games. Splaying means that cards are arranged in a particular fashion, or splayed, to display information or special abilities. Splays can be used in simple situations, like cards showing their values and suits being organized over one another. They can also be used in complex circumstances, like a mystery game that reveals a clue when the cards are aligned just right.

Splaying often operates with melding. Melding is when players lay down cards in groups called melds to earn points. This happens when cards have something in common. For example, a meld could consist of cards all with the same number, or a series of cards with the same suit in numerical order, usually called a run.

Traditionally, players must assemble melds in their hand of cards before laying them down. Some rule variations allow players to alter the melds after having played them. Adding to a meld is often referred to as laying off. Some games even let you lay off cards onto an opponent's meld.

TRICKS

Another common card game mechanic is trick-taking. Each turn, players choose a card from their hand and place it face up in the center of the play area. Typically, the highest card wins the round or trick, though suit type may come into play as well.

When players win a trick, they collect the cards played that round and set them aside. At the end of the round, players receive a score depending on how many tricks they've won. This is a scoring phase initiated by the construct of turns and rounds. Scoring phases may occur through specific gameplay, player accomplishments, or at random. As a game designer, choosing when and how to score can be an interesting spot of creativity.

Just like any other mechanic, there are countless variations. Some trick-taking games deal out every card from the deck at the beginning, while other games limit the number of cards dealt each round. Other variations include a betting phase or a requirement that subsequent players have to follow the lead of the first player's card suit. Some games even include a special suit that outranks all other suits, no matter their value. However the games vary, the ultimate goal is to win the most tricks.

A curious variation on trick-taking asks players to do the exact opposite of normal games. This is often described as trick-avoidance, a reverse game in which the winner actually acquires the fewest tricks and therefore the least points. Hearts is an example of a trick-avoidance game.

A close relative to trick-taking is known as ladder climbing. When in use, players take turns shedding cards from their hands. The first player puts down a single card or a particular set, like a pair, three of a kind, or quads. Then, the following players must play cards of equal or greater value. When a combination of cards is used, like triples, the following players must continue to play triples or forfeit their turn. The last player who plays after all the others have passed gets to go first next round.

In variations, players can pass on their turn, even if they have cards they could legally play. In some games, wild cards are provided that can clear the board, allowing whoever played it to go first in the new round. Ladder-climbing traditionally utilizes a deck of playing cards; often, the 2s are wild, turning the worst cards in the deck into the best.

Generally, the goal is shedding your entire hand, known as going out. Usually, the person who goes out first wins, and the others keep playing to determine second, third, and so on, as in Presidents.

MOVEMENT VIA CARDS

One particular card mechanic, known as move through deck, provides a sense of moving forward without requiring a board or map. Players could flip cards to represent exploring a haunted house or ancient temple, room by room, having random encounters while working their way from the top of the deck to the bottom as if in an interactive story.

Moving components is also a good use for a deck of cards. For example, if you draw a card with a pink location on it, then you would move your game piece to the next available pink location on the board.

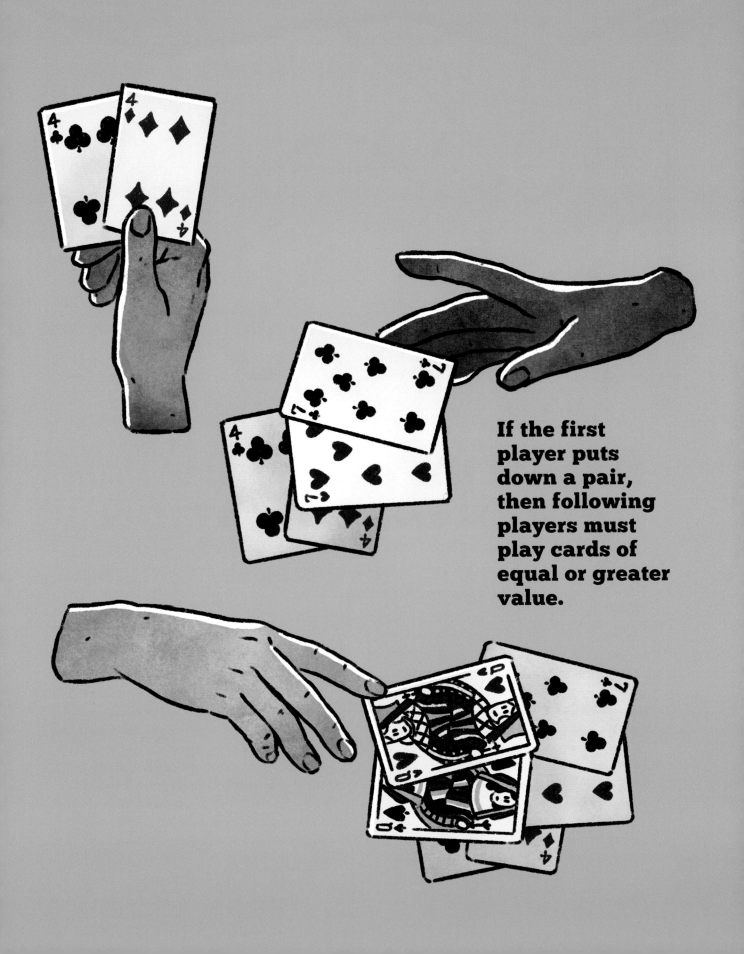

If the first player puts down a pair, then following players must play cards of equal or greater value.

NEGOTIATION & HIDDEN INFORMATION

Negotiation is integral not only to gaming but also to civilized society. In its purest form, it's holding a discussion or interaction in hopes of reaching an agreement.

Negotiation is basic: As children, we learn ways of working out issues like "I cut, you choose" to divide and share a treat. As a mechanic used in gaming, it ensures the person splitting will make it as fair as possible because the other person will likely choose the larger share.

For example, one player may draw multiple cards, examine them, and then divide them into two piles. The other player gets to choose which pile of cards they each get.

Beyond the concept of negotiation is hidden information, the difference between what is known and what is unknown. Hidden information means that one or more players are aware of some secret knowledge, such as a player knowing their hand of cards while their opponents do not. Hidden information is paramount in games of negotiation and plays a large role in many types of games—especially role playing games, where a game master harbors secret knowledge about maps and monsters.

The idea of unknown information goes a step further. It means that no player is aware of the knowledge. For example, players may know which cards are in a deck, but not the order of the cards. Players take a gamble with the limited knowledge that they do have.

TRADING, BRIBING, BLUFFING, AND STEALING

A fundamental form of negotiation is trading, which means that players can make deals with each other concerning their assets. When negotiating a trade, players come to a compromise about a mutual interest, even if sometimes the benefits can appear unbalanced. If a trade is unbalanced, one or both players likely have a hidden agenda.

For example, a player may offer two resources for another player's one, which may seem unequal. Why would a player do this? It's difficult to know when there is hidden information—the player may be holding anything in their hand. Pursue negotiations carefully.

Incentivizing a trade to make it more attractive to your opponent could also be considered a type of bribery. You are requesting that a player make a particular trade by providing a bonus. A bribe can also occur outside of trades. For example, Player 1 could offer payment to Player 2 to attack Player 3.

Bribes can be included in a game's rules, meaning that you must adhere to a bribe once agreed upon. If the rules do not state that you must honor your agreement, then players could bluff. Bluffing can be particularly useful in games that hinge on hidden information.

Besides bribing or trading, there are plenty of games that employ stealing to get what you desire. Just be aware that stealing is a surefire way to make an enemy.

Players can come to a compromise, even if the benefits appear unbalanced.

SIMULTANEOUS ACTION SELECTION

The opposite of such devious negotiation mechanics would be an alliance, which is when players join forces for a mutual benefit. This collaboration is different from team-based games because teams are created at the beginning of a game and remain that way until the end. Alliances can be formed and broken freely, allowing for diplomacy, commitment, betrayal, and surprises. A game's rules will guide these partnerships.

When using simultaneous action selection, actions are planned in secret and revealed at the same time. This can create or break alliances. Players choose their actions, creating an action queue during a secret selection phase. Players can keep their action queue entirely secret, or they can have private discussions with others to make plans. Players resolve their plans in turn order, which is important because your plans may get spoiled by another player's actions ahead of you. Not everything in your action queue may be possible once it's time to play.

It is the designer's responsibility to use a turn order that is fair and gives everyone a chance to act first throughout the rounds, such as a progressive turn order, discussed further in reference to alternating turn orders.

FLIP to pg. 24 for more info!

Turn order with simultaneous action selection can be switched up by applying action speeds. When an action has the highest speed rating, it plays out before all others, taking priority over turn order. It is important to balance this priority with the potential power of the action.

Action speeds could be used in any game, providing an advantage. For example, if monsters with identical stats faced off in a duel, their battle would require a tie-breaker. But, if one had a higher priority action speed, then that monster would get to strike first, gaining an advantage.

Experiment and Test

No mechanism is perfect in all scenarios; there will always be positive and negative features. Be creative—merge mechanisms that have not mixed before. Be balanced—properly test a prototype to be sure that results are not consistently lopsided.

What distinguishes a fun game is making choices that are challenging and rewarding.

ROLE ORDER

The mechanism of role order complements simultaneous action selection. Players secretly select a role that has a built-in priority number. Once players reveal which roles they've chosen, the actions are played out in priority order; therefore, the turn order operates according to the chosen roles and is always in flux. Role order is similar to using action speeds, though more thematic and used only with simultaneous action selection. Action speeds still allow space for turn order and nonpriority actions.

With role order, cards are often used to represent the characters and actions. A drafting mechanic may be used at the beginning of the game to distribute the various cards to players. Each card may be unique or there may be duplicate cards to allow multiple players to use the same roles. Games may bypass drafting to expedite the game and instead pass out the same set of cards to every player at the start of the game. Drafting is discussed further in reference to action drafting.

FLIP to pg. 31 for more info!

A fascinating mechanism that can be applied to role order results in an increased value of the unchosen. This mechanism makes the unchosen options more appealing in the next round by including additional assets. For example, if no one chooses the role card with the action to build, then next round the choice could come with a lumber resource for choosing it. This bonus could continue to increase each turn the action is not chosen.

INDIVIDUALS, ALLIES, OR TEAMS

In some alliances and team-based games, players may share assets, parts, purchases, and territories, while in other scenarios, players may have components of their own. Sometimes allies or teammates can provide unique traits or abilities for one another. Alliances and teams can come in a variety of shapes and sizes: symmetrical (2 vs. 2, 3 vs. 3, or 2 vs. 2 vs. 2) or asymmetrical (2 vs. 3 or 1 vs. all others).

The format of 1 vs. all could mean that a single player is the game master, controlling any number of enemies in the game while other players control individual heroes. It could be a game about an individual escaping a group of hunters or seekers. It could mean that you are doing so well in a game that all other players now want to come after you.

The mentality of individuality is intensified in any game that chooses to employ the kill-steal mechanism. Kill-steal is traditionally used with a semicooperative game structure. Players work toward accomplishing a common goal, though not necessarily as allies. Sometimes the players will directly attack each other while working together.

Ultimately, players strive to be the one who completes the task at hand, such as delivering the final blow to take down a vicious beast. Only the player who completes the task receives a bonus. The kill-steal mechanic can be employed many times throughout gameplay. It may even be used as a phase or way of resolving an issue. Occasionally, this mechanism is utilized in a cooperative setting, and the player who gets to deliver the death stroke is decided among the whole team.

Continues on Next Page ▶

Werewolf:
Hidden Roles & Traitors

You can build alliances or teams in secret, where only some players may know the real alignments of others. This method is present in Werewolf, an excellent game of social deduction, also known as Mafia. It requires no components but does need a game master or moderator to control the game's flow. Moderators secretly assign characters to players, via cards or shoulder taps, utilizing the hidden roles mechanic. There are many variations to the game; for example, villagers may have no distinctive traits, or they may be individual characters with varied abilities.

Once all the hidden roles have been distributed, gameplay progresses in phases split up as night and day. The game starts at night, and the moderator has everyone shut their eyes, as if asleep. The players designated as werewolves, usually two, are told to open their eyes and look for each other. These monsters then decide on a player to kill (eliminate from the game). Once they make their selection, the werewolves close their eyes.

The player chosen as the protector is told to open their eyes next. The protector, a specialized defensive role, gets to choose one person each round to save from the werewolves. Since this is a player elimination game, it provides extra fun to offer roles like the protector, or a role that includes action beyond death, like an oracle who becomes a ghost if killed. All these actions performed during the night are done so in silence and with eyes closed so that the roles aren't revealed to everyone. Player elimination is discussed further in reference to races.

The game master then shifts night into day and tells all the players to open their eyes. Players picked by the werewolves are dead (eliminated), but if the protector chose a player who was also picked by the werewolves, then that player is safe . . . for now.

FLIP to pg. 39 for more info!

During the rest of this phase (daytime), all players discuss which players are werewolves and then negotiate killing them. This is where misdirection and betrayal can occur because the players who are werewolves are voting, just like everyone else. Alliances can form, though they may fall away as accusations go wild like a witch-hunt.

In the end, the werewolves win if they whittle down the amount of non-werewolf players to match the number of werewolves still in play. The werewolves lose if everyone else can remove them from the game.

Werewolf is an example of how traitor games operate. Traitors win when the other players fail. The difficult task is learning every potential role before playing, because players cannot ask questions about their characters after starting the game without giving away their role. This learning curve can sometimes deter potential players even if gameplay is straightforward.

Mechanics

74

Betrayal can occur because werewolves are voting, just like everyone else.

AUCTIONS

A form of simultaneous negotiation among all players is an open auction, an alternate way of exchanging possessions. Players place a bid by shouting out what they are willing to pay for the thing being sold, and the seller chooses the auction winner. No one is needed to run the auction, and there really aren't any rules. This mechanic is rarely used because it is difficult to track everything that is said.

A controlled style of auction that requires a moderator, or an auctioneer, is an English auction. In this format, the auctioneer calls out for bids of a specific value, and players can claim those values or not, regardless of turn order. A player can use their hand, a bidding paddle, or their voice. The values continue to rise, increasing the cost, until all players are done bidding. When there are no more bids, the prize goes to the highest bidder and the auction ends.

When using a Dutch auction, the auctioneer instead starts with a very high price. If no one claims the bid, the auctioneer decreases the cost. As soon as a player is willing to pay the called-out price, they can claim the bid and win. This format is also known as a one-bid auction because it takes only a single bid to end it.

An alternate version of auctions, known as a turn order until pass auction, eliminates the auctioneer. Players can place bids in turn order until they decide to pass because the cost has become too high. A winner is declared when there is one player left who hasn't passed. This auction type could be limited to a once-around auction, letting players have only one chance to place a bid or pass. This avoids prolonged bidding.

Designers could even make the whole thing secret. In a sealed-bid auction, all bids are revealed at the same time, and the highest bidder is the winner.

Some games use bidding to determine turn order and asset allocation. This method is known as a multiple-lot auction, and it moves the game along by providing a bunch of things at once. Players secretly allocate money and place multiple bids on multiple items and opportunities. Once all bids are revealed, purchases are distributed. A multiple-lot auction is similar to a sealed-bid auction but designed for numerous purchases at once.

ROLE PLAYING

The fundamental mechanic of role playing is acting. Players take on the roles of characters. Acting can be as minimal as controlling a character with a few distinctive traits, or it can be the focus of the entire game.

Some games use variable player powers, meaning that each player has a unique action that only they can perform. In other games, characters are more sophisticated, and gameplay allows progression, so players can improve their characters' abilities over time. They may choose from preexisting characters or create them from scratch. Role playing can include as much or as little as the game designer wishes.

Role playing can be as substantial or as minimal as the game designer wishes.

CLASSIC GAMING EXAMPLE
Charades

A well-known game where acting is the entire premise is Charades, which dates back to the early nineteenth century. This competition uses a specific communication limit: Players must act out clues silently. As they act out a specific word or phrase, their partner or teammates guess what it is.

ARE YOU A JANITOR?

NO! IT'S AN AIR GUITAR! SANTANA?

Players must act out clues silently, as their team guesses what they're communicating.

COMMUNICATION LIMITS

Employing a targeted clues mechanism puts a spin on the typical way to convey hints with limited communication. Targeted clues are different than ordinary clues because all players have the opportunity to guess a solution, but the clue-givers want only their own teammates to guess correctly. Those providing clues seek to have some players deduce the word or phrase, but not all players, even though everyone involved has the opportunity to observe.

In this thought-provoking dynamic, the communicators try to offer hints that are both clear and unclear. Sometimes, if no one can guess the answer, or if everyone can guess the answer, then no points are awarded.

When games require players to draw their answers, they are using a paper-and-pencil mechanism. This may sound similar to score-keeping, but paper-and-pencil means more than keeping track of numbers. Paper-and-pencil may include drawings, puzzles, or calculations on paper or a sophisticated scorecard. Basically, players use a writing utensil and a surface, which could be a notepad and a pen, chalk on slate, or something digital.

Characters gain experience to upgrade stats and powers with each level up.

STORYTELLING

Some role playing games (RPGs) incorporate storytelling. Some people love storytelling in gaming while others are intimidated by so much socialization and improvisation. Storytelling games can be diverse: from crafting a short story as a result of rolling image-based dice to pitching products to judges.

Alternatively, the stories could be presented by the game itself, where players choose from provided options after hearing about their situation. Choosing the outcome of a story is known as a narrative choice. This type of interactive epic usually comes in a book format, but it can also operate as a deck of cards.

Most large-scale RPGs use a similar narrative choice dynamic, but the outcome is open-ended. Players are capable of completely formulating their own options (represented by their player characters, or PCs). Expansive narrative RPGs work best with a game master (GM) to keep track of details. They guide and dictate events within the fictional game world, and control non-player characters (NPCs) for the players to interact with, as in Dungeons & Dragons.

PCs are essential to role playing games. Players often take on fantasy or sci-fi characters, portraying races (such as dwarves and gnomes) and classes (such as wizards and warriors). Characters usually begin at level 1 and, during gameplay, gain enough experience to improve their skills and advance to the next level. Improvement may also occur sporadically through the acquisition of special weapons, items, and armor. Games often provide new powers and upgraded stats with each level up.

Adventure RPGs are typically cooperative games with characters working together to achieve goals. Sometimes, though, RPGs play like a semicooperative game. Players progress through the main story together, while each character has separate motivations and can earn personal assets, including extensive wealth like gems and gold. Sometimes their individual goals can conflict in pursuit of an overall victory.

Campaigns are an accumulation of resource material including stories, battles, scenarios, and missions with an ultimate goal at the end. These campaigns act as sequential episodic experiences. They swap in new regions and challenges, establishing unique gameplay within the same game. These expansions are an excellent way to increase replayability.

GUIDELINES FOR OPEN-ENDED GAMEPLAY

Imagination-based role playing games come with a large measure of rules. Designers must try to anticipate every possible outcome to provide consistent gameplay because the game is so open ended.

For example, if characters can jump or fall, then rules are required to determine the difficulty of jumps and how much damage they might take from falling at different heights. The mechanism of stat check resolution is often used in these situations by applying a difficulty factor. Players roll a die and add a relevant stat as a way to modify the result toward success.

For example, suppose a character attempts a jump. If players are using a 20-sided die (d20), the difficulty factor could be that the player must get an 18 or higher. A value this high means that the jump is challenging. The character's stat that most closely relates to jumping could be under the broader term of agility. If the player rolls a 14 and adds their character's agility stat of 5 to

the outcome, then they end up with 19 in total, enough to succeed.

There are some rolls that are low enough (and high enough) to override other factors, called critical hits and failures. A roll of a 1 is a critical failure, even if the player has enough stats and bonuses to clear the difficulty factor in place.

Becoming a Game Master

Game masters often handle the majority of campaign preparation by developing maps, scenarios, and NPCs ahead of time. Being a GM is a huge task, but resources are available. Game designers sell books of resource material, and fellow gamers continuously create homemade versions to share.

Being a GM is fun, controlling the monsters and traps, but also quite a responsibility; you are accountable for sensible gameplay and player inclusion.

With a critical fail, the amount of harm is amplified. In a normal fall, the rule may be: For every 10 feet that a character falls, roll a 10-sided die (d10) and receive that much damage. Due to a critical fail, the harm may be doubled, or added to the roll of a six-sided die (d6), depending on the game and GM.

A critical hit, when players roll a natural 20 on their initial die roll, leads to greater success—such as elegantly jumping and sticking such a perfect landing that the NPC traveling with you is impressed, and honors you with a gold coin. Critical hits and failures are discussed further in reference to probability management.

FLIP to pg. 52 for more info!

When it comes to RPGs, or cooperative games in general, balancing players is important. Avoid skewing the rules so that a single player is able to control the majority of the action. Each player must have a voice and be heard. The GM helps to keep things balanced.

Misplaced Fears

Modern role playing games became popular in the early 1970s. Their popularity provoked fear and even hostility in many people, who believed that RPGs were connected to evil behaviors or witchcraft. In the 1980s, the media exploded with misguided, sensational articles about the supposed dangers of role playing games.

Today it's well known that RPGs promote a litany of positive qualities like socializing with others, increasing your problem-solving skills, fostering creativity, and much more.

SIMULATION

RPGs can provide a simulation of real-life activities. Whether players are trying to navigate a labyrinth while solving puzzles or to swim underwater against the current, role playing can imitate life. On the other hand, the genre of simulation games is traditionally focused on a specific situation, like managing a factory, working in a bakery, or operating a submarine with a crew of others, as in Captain Sonar.

The zone of control allows the controlling game piece to regulate the space around itself.

WARGAMES: NOW AND THEN

It is possible to trace connections from the latest games to the oldest games. Large-scale role playing games are no exception; they were derived from wargames, like Chess, and altered over time.

Character abilities grew in complexity to include stats, like an attack power or a defensive value. The setting changed to include supernatural elements like magical spells and mythical beings. The game pieces (if used at all) were taken off traditional battlefields or game boards and placed into caverns and dungeons.

Game masters were added to run the show, and designers eliminated the notion of winning or losing because games like these have no particular end. Characters can die, and campaigns may conclude, but players can continue with a new character or begin a new campaign.

Modern wargames fall under the vast umbrella of role playing because of the abilities of figurines and the settings of skirmishes. A fascinating mechanism often used in wargames since the 1960s is a zone of control. It creates a region around a game piece that affects opposing figurines if they enter. The zone of control could force the opposing game piece to attack or use extra action points to continue moving. However it plays out, the zone of control allows the controlling game piece to regulate the space around itself.

Another staple of the modern wargame genre is the use of a combat results table (CRT). Typically, CRTs combine statistics from both the attacking and defending parties and die rolls to determine outcomes. The combination brings elements of chance into the conflict, giving the underdog an opportunity at victory. Often, the underdog can achieve victory through clever tactics or pure luck.

What's Old Is Gold

It's important to note that some of today's best games are, basically, modified old games. Don't be afraid to start with something familiar when designing. Customize it into a new game, complete with unique rules, themes, concepts, and gameplay.

Puzzle games push players to use abstract thought.

PUZZLES

All the mechanisms used in gaming challenge a player's ingenuity and knowledge. When it comes to puzzles, these abilities are challenged even further.

Some may consider a jigsaw puzzle to be a game, because you can win when it is complete and it can be considered cooperative, but unlike other games, a jigsaw puzzle has no rules, turns, or actions.

Often, puzzle games push players to use abstract thought—the ability to perceive objects or ideas that are represented symbolically. While this notion can be found throughout gaming, the genres of puzzles and abstract games often take it further. Puzzles can even eliminate a theme altogether and rely on geometric shapes, numbers, shapeless forms, and colors.

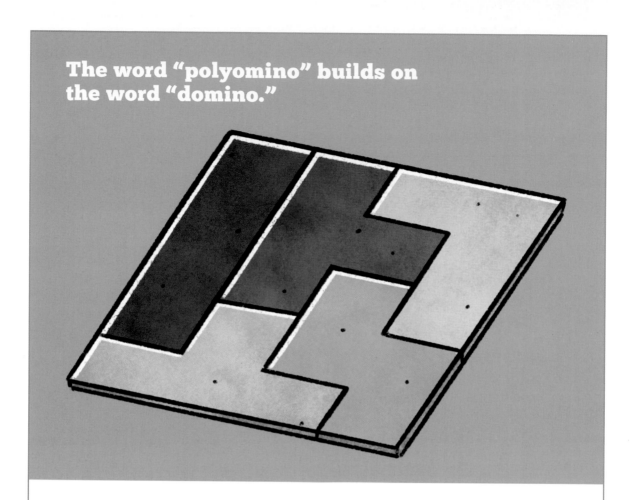

The word "polyomino" builds on the word "domino."

GRID COVERAGE AND POLYOMINOES

A mechanic known as grid coverage is similar to building a jigsaw puzzle, except that there is competition in covering the board. Generally, players are challenged with an assortment of shapes to cover their board as efficiently as possible. Sometimes the layouts affect variables in the game like income and bonuses. It depends on how the shapes are arranged and what spaces they overlay.

Some grid coverage games play out like a race. Players must use the shapes quickly and resourcefully, like trying to maximize space when packing a bag; otherwise, they won't be able to fit everything. Often, there

are benefits to being the first player to cover the grid completely, like in Patchwork.

When dealing with square grids in particular, the components are built out in a tiling fashion, creating polyominoes. (The word "polyomino" builds on the word "domino.") A domino is made of two squares, and a polyomino is an expansion, with more squares and in all different directions. When covering a grid, players need to be wise with their selection. Grid coverage can take place even in three dimensions, further complicating the spatial coordination.

MEMORY AND PATTERNS

A couple of commonly used puzzle mechanics worth noting are memory and pattern recognition. They may include trivia competitions or picking the correct item to complete a series.

EXAMPLE: CONCENTRATION, a.k.a. MEMORY. Concentration can be played with cards or any other components, as long as players can find pairs that are indistinguishable from one another once they're face down (like tiles, tokens, or even shells found on the beach). These components are then laid in a large grid.

Players take turns flipping the components two at a time; if a player reveals a pair, they get to keep it and go again. But, if no pair surfaces, then the components flip back over, and the next player gets to go. At first, players rely on chance to find pairs, but eventually they need to rely on memory to find them before others do.

A memory mechanism that puts added pressure onto players is called speed matching. Generally, the goal is to be the first to spot the match, whether the matching items are similar components or different ones. For example, players may be flipping a card to reveal a pattern and then searching for that same pattern on a prop or token separate from cards.

Pattern recognition comes into play with the mechanism of pattern building. Players accomplish specified goals or gain assets by placing components into particular patterns. For example, if a player manages to set tokens on four even-numbered spaces of a game board in a row, then they get to draw a card.

At first, players rely on chance to find pairs, but eventually they need to rely on memory.

In this "s'more"-themed game, the pieces need to be carefully removed. If it all comes down, the player loses.

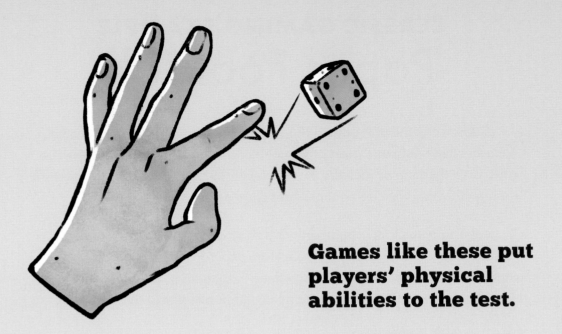

Games like these put players' physical abilities to the test.

PHYSICAL DEXTERITY

Players who are good at throwing and balancing are likely to enjoy games of physical dexterity. They're games for those who want to challenge their skill in steady, nimble precision.

Games like these put players' physical abilities to the test with activities like flicking (hoping to get a game piece to land in a specific zone), stacking and balancing components (taking care to avoid knocking things over), throwing, spinning, and a number of other nimble-fingered actions.

Some games take that physical activity to the next level by asking players to remove pieces from an already balanced structure. If the arrangement comes crashing down, the player involved loses the game. This is a single-loser game: Players aren't attempting to be the best, they merely want to avoid being the worst. It's a mechanic uncommon in modern gaming because of its innate negative structure.

Games can work around a single-loser dynamic by including multiple rounds so that one loss isn't so catastrophic. For example, losing a round could result in a lack of points rather than losing the entire game. If that's the case, then the game uses a score-and-reset system: At the end of each round, players earn points, then return the structure to its default setup, ready for the next round.

You can use physical acts of dexterity in an auction format. For example, to place a bid players could flip a token into a cup from a predetermined distance. There may be a time limit involved, forcing players to play in the moment rather than taking their time to line up shots.

This dexterity auction format causes players to think fast, make a snap decision, and toss their tokens because if they don't make one in, they won't have a bid. All bids are binding, even if the token landed in an unintended spot.

CLASSIC GAMING EXAMPLE
Paper Football

A well-known game that utilizes the flicking mechanism is Paper Football. Players need only one sheet of paper to craft a faux football and play the game. They then tap or flick the paper triangle back and forth across a board or table. (Pushing the component is not allowed.)

The goal is to reach their opponent's end zone, where they earn a touchdown. They then have the opportunity to flick the paper football, aiming to soar across the opponent's fingers, which are held up to look like goal posts. This tricky flicking is similar to kicking a field goal in real-world football.

Paper Football proves that it's possible to create an entertaining game using nothing more than a sheet of paper.

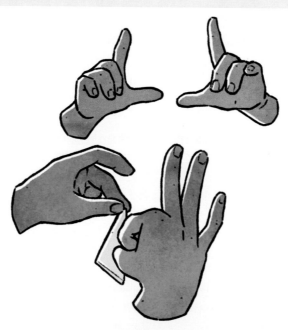

Players earn the opportunity to flick the football, aiming to soar across the opponent's fingers.

VARIABLES

In some games, the structure itself can vary significantly, altering gameplay each turn, round, or play session. When using a variable setup each time you play, you may alternate the maps, starting positions, assets, goals, or other facets of the game.

Game structure can vary significantly each turn, round, or play session.

LEGACY GAMES, RPGS, AND EXPANSIONS

Deciding to alter a game's setup may simply arise from the desires of the players. In other games, variations to setup and gameplay are determined by changes people made to the game the last time it was played. This style of game extends the previous session onto the next, known as a legacy game. The current game builds on players' past actions as well as inherited features from previous games, thus linking the game's past to future sessions yet to be played.

For example, players may write on cards or place stickers on tiles, creating irreversible changes to the game. Some legacy games are resettable: Players can go back to factory defaults because they utilized reusable stickers or added cards that players could remove.

Usually, the goal of a legacy game is to access content by meeting certain conditions, creating changes that remain well beyond a single game. These unlocked alterations can result in vastly different gameplay in the next session, from introducing characters to adding new mechanics.

Some see a legacy game as similar to a role playing game (RPG). In large-scale RPGs, players continually make changes to maps and characters, and these changes remain in future sessions. With legacy games, all the options and alterations come included, built into the game. While some see this as a limitation because it cannot deliver all of the endless options that an RPG can, it can still give you the sense of an ongoing epic. Legacy games provide progression from session to session, without the need for a game master to guide the gameplay.

Legacy games and RPGs are both considered consumable games because of their expendable nature. One-time, solvable mysteries and games like escape rooms are also consumables. Unfortunately, once the puzzle or mystery has been solved, you can't really play it again (unless enough time has passed to forget the outcome).

While many legacy games can still be played after completion, they can lose their appeal. RPGs differ because the game master and players can develop new scenarios and characters. For other games, expansions can fulfill this need. Many games offer expansions that add new content and gameplay without the requirement of learning an entirely different game. RPGs are discussed further in reference to expansion campaigns and storytelling.

FLIP to pg. 79 for more info!

FLIP to pg. 79 for more info!

Legacy games build on players' past actions in previous games.

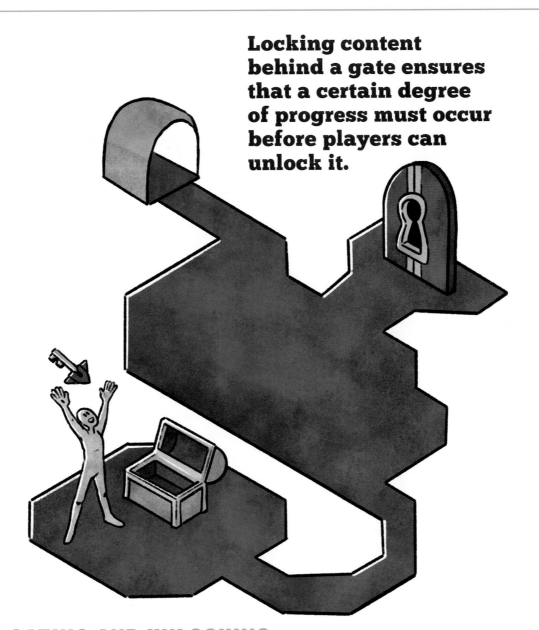

Locking content behind a gate ensures that a certain degree of progress must occur before players can unlock it.

GATING AND UNLOCKING

Designers can devise variable changes that occur within the game and do not modify future sessions. This process of gating and unlocking allows the addition of content midgame. Usually, these changes take place because players have accomplished a goal or reached a checkpoint, or a certain number of rounds have passed.

Gating and unlocking can be viewed as a general switch in gaming. If players fulfill certain requirements, then they create a change in the game. For example, clearing a dungeon can lead you to a key that grants access to a door. Unlocking the door leads to a new map, new characters, and other new game features.

Continues on Next Page ▶

Gating and unlocking is commonly used in worker placement games. A particular building on the game board may require players to unlock it by making space, clearing the land of trees and acquiring lumber. Once players do so, someone still has to spend their action to create the new building, and since all players can use it the task often comes with bonuses. The building could usher in a new age of technology and resources, providing new actions, worker types, and locations.

Locking this content behind a gate ensures that a certain amount of progress must occur before players can unlock it. Gating and unlocking is a gentle way of increasing the complexity of a game over time, without bogging down players immediately with intensive strategy and before mechanics can start to feel stale.

Tech Trees & Tracks

A way of gating and unlocking upgrades for individuals based on personal progress would be to utilize a tech tree or a tech track. These singular advancements often thematically represent new technologies. Players may start with an orchard of apples, then upgrade to a building that can craft cider, diversifying what they can accomplish. Players earn upgrades by paying a specific cost with currency, resources, or some specialized asset created specifically for tech trees.

There are methods of accessing other players' tech trees without earning the upgrades. Some games allow players to pay or trade for the right to use another's tech tree or to take access by force. As a designer, you could choose to have players' control over tech trees expire, allowing others to step

in and claim them or to enable all players to use them once they're unlocked.

Usually, tech tree upgrades have prerequisites, requiring players to obtain first one, then the next available advancement. Let's say you are a general at war controlling a bunch of soldiers, and you want cavalry to improve your attack. To acquire cavalry, your soldiers must first become trained knights, who can then advance to riding horseback.

This advancement is an example of a straightforward upgrade system with a single line of progression, a tech track. In contrast, a tech tree could provide branches of alternate decisions. For example, your soldiers could become knights that could then decide on whether to become cavalry or elephantry, riding on a war elephant instead of a horse.

Sometimes, games employ a literal path to represent each player's progress, using track movement. A token's placement on the track signifies how far players have advanced.

DEPARTURE FROM THE NORM

Many games present variations on how players choose and use actions. One such mechanic, known as action retrieval, grants players a pool of choices they may select from until the pool runs dry. Each player has their own pool of actions, and their retrieval often has its own cost. Action retrieval is like using a deck of cards: After each action is used, it is discarded. You cannot get those actions back until the discard pile is shuffled back into the deck—or in this case, retrieved and returned to your pool.

The cost of action retrieval may be another action, or possibly an entire turn. The card game Hibernation adapts a variation of this process into deck-building. Action retrieval is the trigger for shuffling the discard pile back into the deck instead of traditional deck exhaustion.

Classic deck-builders use cards; designers who want to shake things up could use the mechanic of bag building. In this modification, players use a component other than cards that can be mixed up in a bag and pulled out at random. These could be tiles, tokens, chits, or dice. The shapes must all be similar for this to work. Otherwise, players could identify a component by feeling it.

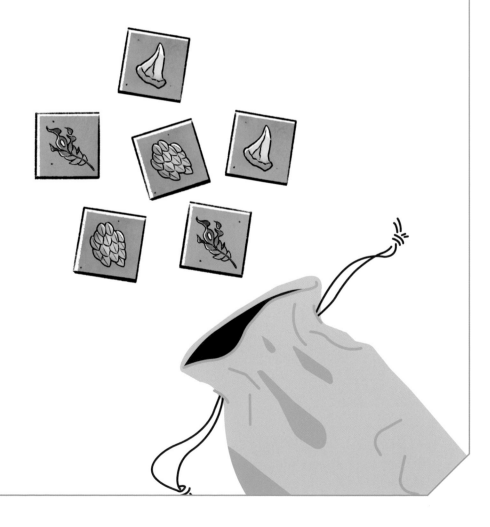

CARD PLAY

An intriguing mechanism that can create a combination of effects is card play. It allows players to use the cards in their hand to modify a situation or outcome. Sometimes card play is constructed into a game as a required phase, or gamers may be able play these cards as interrupts. This card play modification acts as a hidden element, surprising the opponent once it is revealed.

For example, in wargames, the figurines often have base stats that determine who ought to win the conflict. With card play, however, the outcome of the battle can change. The opponent may hold a card that could boost their stats or provide unique abilities. In these situations, players are aware that the outcome can change, because the choice to play a card is included in the gameplay and can occur only during the provided phase. In games that treat card play as an interrupt, players are not aware if and when a card will be played.

Use strategy to get your opponent to use up their cards on false targets first. This strategy may get your opponent to play their only interrupt on a less worrisome component, after which you play the ace up your sleeve.

As an interrupt, card play is given priority over other gameplay, by either opposing or enhancing an action just used. Interrupts can occur immediately at any given time, in response to an action. This means that the latest interrupt must be dealt with first before returning to the action.

Here's an example of an interrupt. A player attacks an opponent. The opposing player raises a defense, using a magical tidal wave action in an attempt to block the attack. The attacking player immediately plays an interrupt card from their hand, called "grow gills," which allows them to get through the water-based defense of the tidal wave and successfully attack the defender. The interrupt card, "grow gills," was essential in getting the attack to go through as planned.

Alternatively, if the defending opponent had chosen not to defend for whatever reason, then the attacker could have used card play to boost the strength value of the unopposed attack. The strength-boosting card could enhance the force of an undefended attack. This is a clever way of approaching an opponent: Make yourself appear weaker than you really are, and then surprise them with hidden force. Interrupts are discussed further in reference to turn order.

FLIP to pg. 27 for more info!

Player 1 approaches with a card worth 5 points.

Player 2 guards with a card worth 7 points.

Player 1 plays an Interrupt card that gives their card +3 points.

Interrupt cards can alter outcomes. Player 1 defeats Player 2 in this conflict.

ACTION / EVENT

An intriguing mechanism that provides players with a choice is known as action or event. Often in the form of a card, the action or event options are presented together and the player can pick one. If the player chooses action, gameplay progresses normally. Choosing action means that the player either receives action points to use later or plays an action now. For example, a player choosing action may receive three action points or move their component and collect a resource.

If the player chooses event, then normal gameplay is interrupted. Events often affect all players. An event could be an intense heatwave, forcing everyone to immediately provide extra water to their crops or risk losing them, or it could be that the player currently in the lead receives a bonus. Events can be harmful or beneficial. This is an area for creativity within your own game. In some situations, if a player doesn't select the event, then opposing players can choose the event. Allowing choice is interesting because events are traditionally out of a player's control.

Designers may devise a way to let players know particular events are coming. For example, players may be warned of a coming tornado by particular cloud formations. An event deck of cards could be stacked so that a special cloud formation card is drawn before a tornado card every time. If players don't get their game pieces into safe locations, then they will be in danger during the oncoming storm. Event decks are discussed further in *Rain Toads*.

FLIP to pg. 116 for more info!

One way to determine the end of a game is with a fixed number of events. The game is over once an event is played a specific number of times. A fixed number of events can be used as a game-ending condition and a game-winning condition. For example, the game may end after the third flood, and the player who initiated the most floods could be the winner. In a different game, the winner could be the person with the most victory points, not the player who initiated the most floods.

WINNING

It's important that a game has clear ending and winning conditions. Some games conclude with the bell of a timer or the exhaustion of a component, while others end with a goal achieved.

One of the most basic forms of victory is by achieving the most points. Nowadays they are often referred to as victory points, and players can earn them in a variety of ways. Victory points are either gained from meeting a game's conditions or directly through the action of a player.

Receiving victory points from player actions is as simple as it sounds: Specific actions are rewarded with victory points. Simply purchasing a building by spending resources could earn a player a permanent victory point. And permanent victory points are also as simple as they sound: They belong to a player permanently.

Victory points can also be obtained by accomplishing specific conditions. This means that you meet a set of requirements, like being the first person to connect three locations together. Doing so could earn you a permanent point, or it may be a temporary victory point, requiring you to defend it thereafter by always having the most locations connected.

Temporary points cannot be guaranteed until a scoring phase or the end of the game has been reached. When temporary victory points can swing back and forth between players in this way, it's like a tug-of-war. Scoring phases are discussed further in reference to trick-taking.

FLIP to pg. 68 for more info!

A basic form of victory is achieving the most points.

TUG-OF-WAR

A strange game-ending and game-winning condition is known as tug-of-war. Universally recognized, tug-of-war is a game of physical strength, where individuals or teams on each side of a rope tug until they overwhelm the opposing party. This mechanism is symbolically the same in gaming: When opponents are overwhelmed, the game is won, or the victor can simply trigger events or earn points instead. It all depends on how the mechanism is used.

The tug-of-war mechanism often translates to board gaming as a track. The game utilizes track movement, but instead of representing each player with individual markers, only one marker is needed. Each player owns an equal portion of the track, and the marker indicates how far away it has moved from the neutral center position. Once it reaches the end of a player's track, it triggers an event, the scoring of points, or total victory.

For example, the marker may advance along the track toward the player who draws

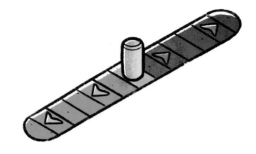

a particular kind of card, such as a cow card. When Player 1 draws a cow card, the marker moves away from the neutral position one space toward Player 1's end of the track. Then, Player 2 draws a cow card, and the marker moves back to neutral. When Player 2 draws a second cow card, the marker is advanced one space farther, now heading toward Player 2's end.

An exciting way to use this mechanism is to offer it as an alternative win condition. One player may be focusing on the tug-of-war as a side path to victory, while their opponent focuses on the main victory approach, drawing only enough cards to prevent the other from reaching their end of the track.

Multiple Tug-of-War

The tug-of-war mechanic is even more fascinating when used with more than two players. Each player still owns a path, but there could be three, four, five, or any number of them extending out from the neutral position in the center. There's still only one token needed, but the marker can progress on any track.

When halting an opponent's progression and working the token back toward your track, it first works away from the opponent's finish line and toward the neutral position before working its way up your own path.

ENDGAME AND BEYOND

Some victory points are granted at the end of the game, known as endgame bonuses. A player does not win these points until after the competition has ended and after a final scoring phase. This setup often provides a surprise and can turn the tides for the losing player. Endgame bonuses are discussed further in reference to *Intergalactic Laboratory*.

FLIP to pg. 120 for more info!

It's important to recognize that games are not only about earning points. Conclusion and victory can be reached by either scoring the most points or by completing specific conditions of the game. This is well illustrated in Chess: Achieving checkmate is a victory condition.

HIGHEST-LOWEST

A curious variation on game-ending mechanics is the highest-lowest method, which encourages balance among each player's assets. Players collect several types of assets, and at the end of the game the winner is determined by counting the lowest asset of each player. Whichever player has the higher quantity of lowest assets wins. In other words, players are awarded a victory point for each one of their lowest assets.

For example, perhaps players are collecting insects, such as caterpillars, grasshoppers, and fireflies. If Player 1's lowest asset is fireflies, because they have only 3, but Player 2's lowest asset is caterpillars, with 4, then Player 2 wins because their highest-lowest asset was 4, earning 4 victory points. When in combination with the concept of hidden victory points, it can be challenging to know how many assets an opponent has and what you should focus on collecting or producing. This format causes players to balance their asset growth evenly.

Whichever player has the greater quantity of lowest assets wins.

CIRCUIT BREAKER

It can be possible to end games early with a circuit breaker if you've achieved such dominance that your victory is inevitable. Similar to the circuit breakers in the electrical panel in your home, this mechanism has the power to end the game, crowning a winner. A circuit breaker offers an alternative conclusion in case the game becomes lopsided with no hope of returning to a balance.

For example, a circuit breaker could be added to Chess that allows a player to win if they manage to capture every one of the opponent's pawns.

A circuit breaker can also be an alternative path to victory that a player may pursue instead of the main objective. For example, in a game where the objective is to capture the most fish using worms as bait, there may be a circuit breaker that applies if a player collects 20 worms. Halfway through gameplay, Player 1 has six fish and Player 2 only has one fish, but Player 2 collected 20 worms. Because the circuit breaker has occurred, the game is over, and Player 2 is champion. Utilizing a tug-of-war lends itself well to the circuit breaker mechanism as it's a distinct way of representing which player is in the lead, and by how much.

A circuit breaker can work as a contingency plan, but using such a mechanic could mean that the game itself is unbalanced. Be sure to playtest your game thoroughly. It's essential that it feels like the circuit breaker belongs logically or at least thematically, and that it's not a quick fix for slow or complicated gameplay.

TIE-BREAKER

If the game ends with a tie among players, then a tie-breaker must decide the true champion. There are many ways to determine the winner of a tie. The winner may be the person who obtained the most assets or components throughout the game.

Alternatively, the winner could be the person with the least amount of resources, meaning the winner is the most efficient player. A game's rules could also leave the tie-breaker up to randomization by simply rolling the highest on a die or drawing a stronger card than your opponents.

A tie-breaker is an effective tool both at the end of a game and also throughout gameplay. To determine the outcome of ties that occur while in-game, you may compare the stats of a character or component, such as speed, health, or size. Some players may even use thumb wrestling to quickly determine a tie that has occurred during gameplay.

Sudden Death

A popular tie-breaker is sudden death. In the event of a tie, additional rounds are played to determine the winner. The first person who wins the next point, territory, asset, or entire round is officially the victor.

Sudden death usually occurs at the end of a tie game, but players can call for it early, if there is no time left to finish. This particular scenario may occur at the end of a siesta or recess. Sudden death is discussed further in reference to *Intergalactic Laboratory*.

FLIP to pg. 120 for more info!

CLASSIC GAMING EXAMPLE
Rock-Paper-Scissors

Another traditional way of breaking a tie is to play Rock-Paper-Scissors. Not only is it quick and easy, but it's also a great game. Rock-Paper-Scissors is component free, and there is no predicting your opponent (unless they are transparent or repetitive).

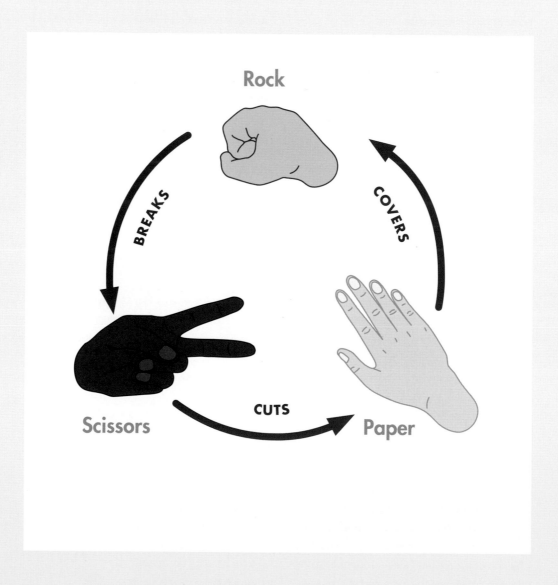

FINALE

A mechanism that may sound similar to sudden death is a finale, which starts a mini-game once the main phases of a game have concluded. This occurs at the end of a game, no matter what, while sudden death happens only under certain circumstances. Players who succeed throughout the game may be awarded an advantage for the mini-game based on assets or stats.

Finales can employ mechanics and gameplay that differ significantly from the main game. Occasionally, this can take away from the experience of a game when victory is dependent on a different mini-game in the end. Keep in mind that it can be quite disappointing for players to lose the finale after having done so well throughout the rest of the game.

TRANSITIVE & INTRANSITIVE RELATIONSHIPS

Rock-Paper-Scissors helps to demonstrate multiple interesting gaming theories. First, the three options available to players have an intransitive relationship, meaning that they are superior to each other in rotation, like a circle. Rock beats scissors, scissors beats paper, and paper beats rock.

This is in opposition to many games that use a transitive relationship based on numerical values. For example, stat-based attacks: If Hydras defeat Archers and Archers defeat Dölgins, then Hydras defeat Dölgins.

Hydra Wins!   **Archer Wins!**

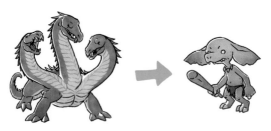

Hydra Wins!

ZERO-SUM OR NOT

Another fascinating concept is the zero-sum game, in which every win is evenly correlated by a loss. Rock-Paper-Scissors is a great example of this type of game. When you play rock and beat your opponent's scissors, you have won a match, and they have lost. The only way that you could win is for them to lose. This theory holds true in most wargames, like Checkers and Chess: To win the game, you must take down your opponent.

The theory of zero-sum is not limited to the winning or losing of an entire game. This win-or-lose outcome could occur multiple times within a single match. For example, if there is a particular location on the board that is clearly the best, then everyone is probably competing to obtain it. Only one player can own the prime location; all others cannot.

In a non-zero-sum game, multiple players can win and lose without affecting one another. It's common in many games: Players can earn points as a result of completing specific actions or accomplishing sets of conditions. Generally, earning points does not deprive others of points.

To Sum It Up . . .

Often games require both zero-sum and non-zero-sum mechanics. If there are no zero-sum situations, games can end up feeling like a solo venture, because there's no way to interact with your opponents. And if a match is made up of only zero-sum situations, then it may turn off some of your players, because some can feel personally threatened when attacked without mercy on a game board.

When testing your games, keep an eye on the mood of the players. Are they bored? Maybe there are too many non-zero-sum situations. Are they frustrated? Maybe too many zero-sum.

CLASSIC GAMING EXAMPLE
Chess

In Chess, the ultimate goal is to capture the king, although you will also need to seize other components along the way. Chess uses the replacement technique for this: The attacking game piece takes the place of the game piece that it has captured. You'll attempt to surround the opposing king and reduce his movement to only those moves that will result in his downfall. When the king is susceptible to capture, it is called a check, but when the king is unable to escape capture, it is called a checkmate, and the game ends.

INFANTRY, CAVALRY, ELEPHANTRY, AND CHARIOTRY

The oldest version of modern Chess traces back to about 600 CE in northwest India, though it is likely much older. It was called Chaturanga, which roughly means "army," but more specifically refers to the classical Indian army that consisted of four branches: the infantry (foot soldiers), cavalry (soldiers on horseback), elephantry (soldiers riding war elephants), and chariotry (soldiers driving chariots).

You will need to seize components along the way to capturing the king, using the replacement technique.

GAME CRAFTING

This chapter presents you with four vastly different, highly **customizable games**, in order from simplest to most complex. Here you will learn how to build a game and its rulebook. This is the culmination of the book, incorporating all the elements previously discussed into these four games.

Think of them as recipes that break a game down to its base ingredients and the steps involved. They can act as your guide until you are ready to create from scratch, without a recipe, a game of your very own.

CATCH THE SPARK

Creating a tabletop game is almost like crafting a universe. You're building a world of rules and components, goals and outcomes. As a designer, you decide what can happen and how.

When you feel ready and motivated, begin crafting something unique. Draw inspiration from what fuels you, excites you, or interests you. Be inspired by the media you love, such as books, movies, television shows, or anything else. They can provide exciting concepts that may drive you to incorporate particular mechanics.

INSPIRATIONS

If you love a book about wizards and the potions they concoct, you might include a deck of cards full of sorcerous resources. The deck might include the items needed for a magical concoction, such as the feather of a phoenix, a werewolf's tooth, and snake scales. Once players have collected the items, they could trade in the set of resources for a card that represents the potion.

The potion card could be used as an interrupt. Players could choose to trigger it at any given time, activating some unique action, just like drinking a potion. Maybe it allows the player to breathe fire, countering any just-played card by sending it to the discard pile.

Games can reflect the activities you enjoy. Perhaps you love to garden. You could craft a worker placement game in which players are planting crops. Players must strategize when caring for their plants. For example, maybe every few turns a swarm of pests arrives; players must grow the proper crops to deter those pests or they will lose their harvest.

You may be inspired by other games (all designers are). Like Hearts or Mancala, which have multitudes of variations, games are rarely completely original inventions. Games are more like evolutions as crafters modify and recombine the rules, components, and themes. While designing games requires loads of creativity and ingenuity, sometimes newer games can feel almost like a product of communal creation, like folk stories that change with each telling.

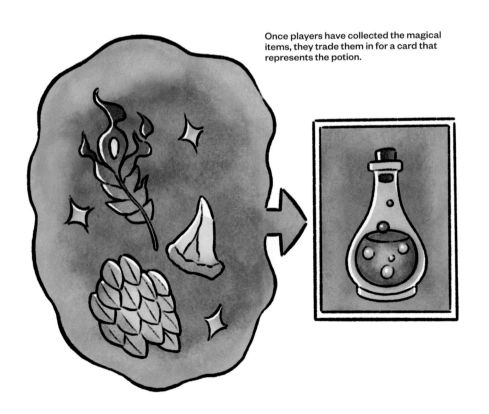

Once players have collected the magical items, they trade them in for a card that represents the potion.

READY, SET . . .

Where to begin? You may first decide on the components, game-play, and rules, then work in mechanics that make the most sense. Or you may start with mechanics and work the components, game-play, and rules around them. There's no right or wrong order.

For example, if you really love the mechanics of physical dexterity, particularly flicking, start there. Then apply a concept that makes thematic sense. If you love star gazing, then the flicking could represent gods sending shooting stars across the sky.

If you're short on components, you can craft a makeshift game board out of soil or sand by digging small pockets or drawing lines. For game pieces, try using rocks or small pine cones. See if you can fashion your own lots (primitive dice) from natural objects. Sticks and stones may break your bones, but they make great components.

Apply a concept to flicking that makes thematic sense, like sending shooting stars across the sky.

Sticks and stones may break your bones, but they make great components.

Tips I've Learned the Hard Way

- If you have an idea you like, **run with it**. Craft the components needed and test it out. You may have to guess at first. For example, when deciding how many spaces should be on a game board, start sketching. If you end up with 20 spaces because that's just the way things fit, try it out.

- Try not to get immediately **hung up** on the end goal.

- Focus at first on a **small feature** of your game, defining what you want most to happen. Add elements as your creation grows in complexity, or keep it simple, fast-paced and focused with few tasks.

- When putting your game together, don't feel pressured to create every single component. You're likely to have useful items around the house. **Borrow dice, props, resources, and tokens** from other games. After all, you're developing a prototype.

- Once you've established a game that is playable and fun, **playtest it** with friends and family, or alone if need be, to ensure that it is functioning as intended without strange anomalies.

- Don't let a failed attempt slow you down; instead, **learn from it**. What is it about the rule that didn't work? How could it be made to work? Does it work with two players but not with four?

15 MINUTES   2 PLAYERS   AGES 8+

Duely Noted is a painless introduction to game design. With a limited number of mechanics and choices, it is fast-paced and easy to understand.

As a bonus, it gives you a basic understanding of how to read music and a fun review of mathematics. Players learn about the different types of notes and their values, and when and where they can use them. The values of the notes teach fractions.

COMPONENTS

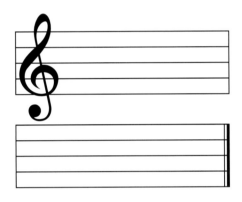

BOARD
2 bars

TOKENS
5 victory points

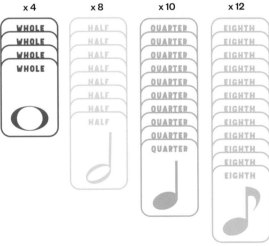

CARDS
4 whole notes, 8 half notes,
10 quarter notes, and 12 eighth notes

Rules

GOAL: Players aim to be the star by playing the most notes on the musical staff. The staff has two bars, or measures. The most you can play per bar is a whole note or a combination that equals a whole, making it complete.

For example, someone could play a half note, the following player a quarter note, and the last player could complete the bar by playing another quarter note. A half plus two quarters equals a whole. Once two bars are completed, the player with the most notes on the entire musical staff earns a victory point.

PREP: Players may want to sit on the same side of the game board so that everyone can easily read it. Shuffle the deck of cards. Then, deal five cards to each player, which becomes their hand of cards. Finally, gather tokens to represent the victory points.

STARTING PLAYER: The player who most recently played an instrument or sang a song gets to take their turn first.

GAME END: The first player to obtain three victory points wins the game.

TURN OVERVIEW: Each turn, players may either play a card or draw a card. When there are no more cards to be drawn, shuffle the discard pile and it becomes the new deck.

When playing a card, each player should place it on a different line on the staff to help show whose cards are whose. Once the bars fill with the proper value of notes and a victory point is awarded, clear the board of cards and place them into the discard pile. This process starts a new round, each player draws two cards to add to their hand, and turns proceed as normal.

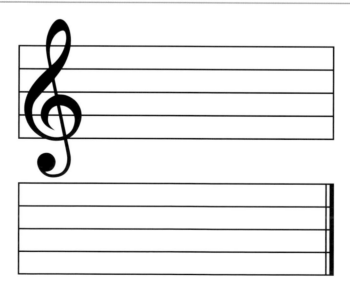

The staff has two bars. When playing notes on the staff, each player should place their card on a different line. The double bar indicates the end.

Steps

1 Play a card or draw a card.

2 If both bars have filled with notes that add up to equal a whole, then award a victory point to the player with the most notes in total.

3 If there is a tie for the most notes, neither player receives a victory point.

4 Clear the board. Each player draws two cards, and the next round begins.

Exceptions & Explanations

If players tie for the most notes on the staff, no one gets a victory point that round. Clear the staff of notes and begin again.

Customize It!

Smaller Fractions. Try adding more notes to the deck. With 16th notes, or even 32nd notes, the rounds would be longer because you'd have more choices. This would require a different strategy. It could also become more challenging to draw the card that you're looking for because there are more cards in total.

You must add an even number of cards. Players need to be able to complete the bar, and they can't if there is an odd number of a type of note or not enough of them. If there are only a couple of 16th note cards in the deck, players may be drawing for quite a while until they find the only note that can complete the bar. You could add 16 of the 16th note cards to the deck, or at least eight to start.

Power Draw. Instead of merely drawing or playing on your turn, provide another option. When players choose Power Draw, they can both draw and play, but they must also discard two cards as a cost.

It's a gamble to shed two in hopes of getting the one that you need, but it can also avoid an entire turn of only drawing and not placing any cards on the bar. With this rule, you can have the best of both worlds, drawing and playing—with an attached sacrifice.

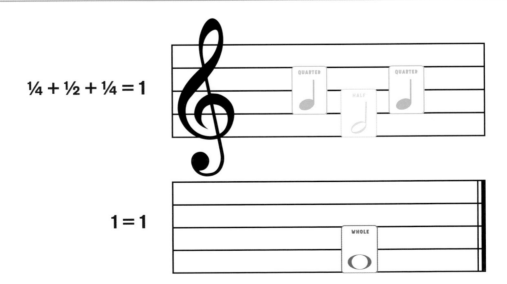

$$\frac{1}{4} + \frac{1}{2} + \frac{1}{4} = 1$$

$$1 = 1$$

Play notes left to right, top bar to bottom. If there's a tie, no one gets a point. Clear the staff, each player draws two cards, and turns proceed as normal.

RAIN TOADS

20-45 MINUTES   2-4 PLAYERS   AGES 9+

Rain Toads can feel like a race, but it is truly all about ownership. The toads in the local pond want to purchase as many lily pads as possible and become real-estate moguls. They earn cash by circling the game board and returning to the Feeding Pad. Players strive to move faster than their opponents so they can earn more coins and buy more lily pads.

Rain Toads uses currency called Croak Coins. Players must be cautious when crossing the Predator Zone, and the event deck keeps the game interesting with a possible deluge of rain every round.

COMPONENTS

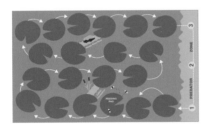

BOARD
Lily pond

GAME PIECES
4 toads

CARDS
Event deck of 15 Sun and 5 Rain cards

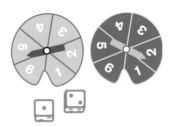

DICE/SPINNERS
2 d6 or 2 lily pads

CURRENCY
30 Croak Coins

TOKENS
4 uniquely colored sets of 10 ownership tokens

Rules

GOAL: Players compete to own the most lily pads while struggling through the rainy season.

PREP: Scour through the event deck and find the five Rain cards plus two Sun cards. Set them aside, then separate the deck into two piles.

Put two Rain cards into one pile and three in the other. Shuffle them separately, and stack one pile on top of the other. Put one of those reserved Sun cards on the very top and another one on the bottom. That becomes the event deck.

Set up the board. Set aside the Croak Coins in one pile (representing the Croaker Broker/bank), and the ownership tokens into separate piles for each player. Place your game pieces on the board. All players start at the Feeding Pad.

STARTING PLAYER: Whoever has most recently interacted with a frog or toad gets to go first. Turns progress clockwise in a fixed order.

GAME END: The game concludes after the fifth Rain card is drawn. Players complete that round plus one more. After the final round, the player with the most lily pads wins.

TURN OVERVIEW: At the beginning of each round, reveal a card from the event deck. This card determines the weather for that round. If it's a Sun card, then turns progress as usual. But if it is Rain, then all players on the board are washed from their spaces and carried to the Feeding Pad.

➡ Any time you start your turn on the Feeding Pad, including your first turn, you receive two Croak Coins. You can either roll the dice and move or choose to Rain Dance, which lets you pull another event card for this round. When rolling, players use two dice but choose the one result they prefer (dice selection).

➡ If you land on an available space, you may pay one Croak Coin to purchase it and place an ownership token on the lily pad. If your game piece lands on an opponent's purchased space you may buy it out from under them for triple the price, three Croak Coins. The Croaker Broker has got to get paid.

➡ If you land on a space that's connected to another by a shortcut, Mossy Rock Pass, or Cattail Connection, then you may use it to move your game piece to the connected space. This shortcut can be used only if you land on the connecting space; you cannot be passing by. You do not have to take the path; you can stay put and potentially purchase that space.

➡ If you end your turn in the Predator Zone, move your game piece off the board. When your turn comes back around, roll the dice. If one of them is a six, then your toad returns to the Feeding Pad. Go again. If neither is a six, you lose your turn. Remain in the Predator Zone until your next turn.

You do not have to take shortcuts; instead you can purchase the space you land on.

Steps

1 As a precursor phase to each round, draw an event card. If it's a Sun card, then continue as usual. If it's Rain, then send all players back to the Feeding Pad. Now, each player may go.

2 If at the start of your turn you're on the Feeding Pad, collect two Croak Coins.

3 If at the start of your turn you're removed from the board, roll two dice. If you receive a six, then place your game piece on the Feeding Pad and start your turn over (go back to step 2).

4 Roll two dice to move around the board, or Rain Dance. If rolling, choose one outcome and move that many spaces. If Rain Dancing, draw another event card and play it out.

5 You may take a shortcut if possible.

6 You may purchase a lily pad if possible.

7 If at the end of your turn you're in the Predator Zone, remove your game piece from the board.

Exceptions & Explanations

You can buy only the spaces that you've landed on. The Feeding Pad cannot be bought. When approaching the Feeding Pad, you may force your game piece to end its move there to receive Croak Coins next turn. You cannot receive Croak Coins for merely passing by the Feeding Pad. You cannot force your game piece to stop its movement anywhere else on the board.

Customize It!

Pond Expansion. The provided game board is an example of a tested prototype that works within the given rules. As a designer, develop a radically different board. Maybe yours has twice as many spaces, with more shortcuts. Perhaps the Predator Zone has fewer spaces, or more.

More Events. The event deck is a way to provide a clear ending to the game, plus some exciting incidents during gameplay. Expand on this notion. Perhaps more weather conditions can spice up life in the lily pond. You could add Snow, Hail, Monsoon, or Thunderstorm cards to the pile, each with unique effects. You could even add more Sun cards to lengthen the overall game.

Slowed Movement. During a Rain event, you may want the deluge to slow the toads' movement. To do this, provide only one die to players on their turn instead of two, until the next round when the sun comes out. When players cannot choose a better outcome between the two dice, they must take what they can get as they slog through the storm.

Leaf Umbrella. Perhaps in exchange for a Croak Coin, players may create a Leaf Umbrella to avoid being sent back to the Feeding Pad by the rain. This option could be presented to players after drawing a Rain event card, but before the rain washes them back to the Feeding Pad and anyone begins their turn.

The Leaf Umbrella could last until the end of the round, dissolving in the downpour so players would have to make a new one when the rain comes again. Using this rule in conjunction with Slowed Movement could be interesting, because a Leaf Umbrella could negate Slowed Movement's effects.

INTERGALACTIC
LABORATORY

45-90 MINUTES

2-4 PLAYERS

AGES 10+

Intergalactic Laboratory is a worker placement game in which you can utilize many assets and earn victory points. Players send their robot workers into mines to collect resources. They can use those resources to build more robots in the Lab, extend conduit (power lines) out to new locations, and build more mines or tree farms.

The tree farms require a specialized ultraviolet (UV) robot worker to grow saplings. Eventually, the trees will transform the planet to resemble Earth, a process called terraforming.

COMPONENTS

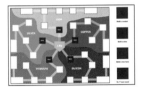

BOARD
Planet surface

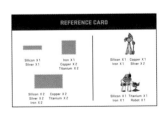

GAME PIECES
4 uniquely colored sets of
7 robot workers and 4 UV robot workers

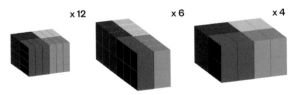

TOKENS
4 uniquely colored sets of
12 conduits, 6 mines, and 4 tree farms

CARDS
5 unique resource card decks and a sapling
card deck—7 of each card (create more as needed)

DIE/PAPER & PENCIL
1 d20 or a writing utensil and surface

PROP
Reference card

INSTRUCTIONS

Rules

GOAL: Build an empire of robots and locations. Be the player with the most victory points at the end.

PREP: Set up the game board and provide players with their color choice of components: conduits, mines, tree farms, robots, and UV robots. Each player may use only one regular robot to start and must build everything else.

Set aside the resource cards and sapling cards in individual piles, as the bank.

Check the reference card for costs of constructing conduits, mines, tree farms, and robots.

STARTING PLAYER: The person who most recently observed the stars gets to play first.

GAME END: Complete 20 rounds. Tally up the scores of each player, counting only permanent victory points. This includes 1 point per robot (including UV robots), 1 point per mine, and 2 points per tree farm.

➡ **In the case of a tie,** begin sudden death! Keep playing one round at a time, checking the score after each. The game ends when, at the end of any sudden death round, one player has the most victory points.

➡ **Now the endgame bonuses** come into play. They include 2 points per accomplishment to the people with the most conduits, UV robots, and saplings. Add the bonuses to the current point count to determine the victor.

TURN OVERVIEW: Players place a worker on a space, and the space indicates what the worker can do. Only one worker can occupy a mine round tree farm per round. On spaces that allow you to build, one worker per player may erect something each round.

Unlike on the spaces that allow you to build, only one worker may claim going first next round.

➡ One location lets players claim going first next round, and only one worker in total may be placed here (claim turn order). When turn order then alternates, always continue clockwise from the new first player.

➡ As long as players have available workers (robots and UV robots), they may continue taking turns, until they have no more workers to play and the round ends. If it's a player's turn and they have no more workers, but others do, they miss that turn.

→ The spaces on the board where players can build are different in size and shape. Conduits are small, thin rectangles, mines are square, and tree farms are large rectangles. Once any conduit, mine, or tree farm is on the board, any player can use it.

→ The lab and its directly connected mines don't need to be placed; they are already provided on the board. To create a new mine or tree farm on the board, a conduit must be linked back to one of the original mines. Once any conduit, mine, or tree farm is on the board, any player can use it.

→ At any point during the game, players may negotiate trades for resources.

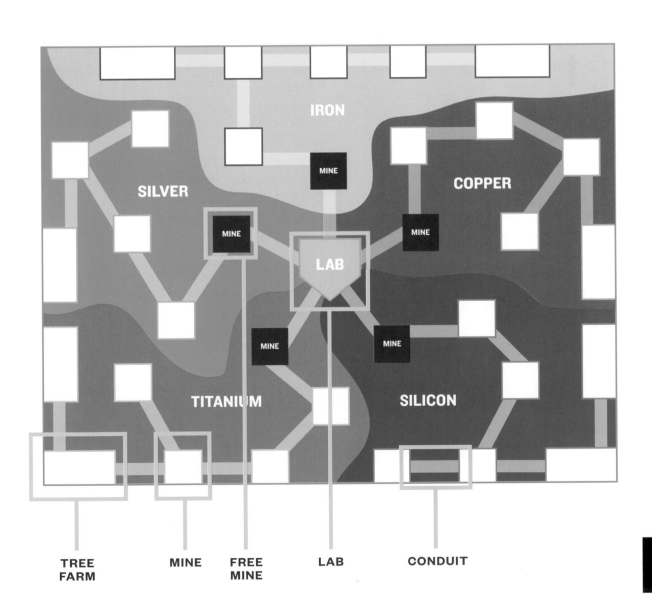

TREE FARM MINE FREE MINE LAB CONDUIT

Steps

1 At the beginning of each round, turn the 20-sided die (d20) to the next number. If you aren't using a die, don't forget to note which round it is on paper.

2 Return all workers to their respective owners.

3 Players take turns in order.

4 If you have a basic robot worker available, place it on a location. The Lab, the surrounding five mines, and "Go 1st next round" space are available at the game's start. The three building spaces are open and available, though you cannot build without first acquiring the necessary resources.

➡ If you place it on a mine, then collect a resource.

➡ If you place it on a space to build a new conduit or mine, then pay the necessary resources and add that component to the board.

➡ If you place it on the Lab location to build a new robot, then pay the necessary resources and build it for immediate use. To build a UV robot in the Lab, your basic robot is part of the cost, and you swap it out for the new worker. You receive the upgraded robot next round.

5 If you have a UV robot worker available, then you have additional abilities. A UV robot can build a tree farm or collect a sapling by placing it on a tree farm. A regular robot worker cannot do either of these things.

6 The game ends once the final round concludes.

7 Calculate scores. If there is a tie, initiate sudden death until one player is leading at the end of the round.

8 Add endgame bonuses. The player with the most points wins.

Exceptions & Explanations

Generally, only one worker in total can occupy any space on the board. The exceptions are the spaces that allow players to build (including the Lab), which can harbor one worker per player.

Only UV robots can interact with the tree farms, meaning building and collecting. A regular robot can build the conduit that leads to the tree farm, but not the farm itself. Regular robots also can't collect saplings.

In addition, UV robots can do anything that an ordinary robot worker can do, because a regular robot was required in the cost. Be aware, the upgrade to a UV robot also requires time, so you do not immediately receive it for use, unlike everything else you build and collect. The new UV robot becomes available for use at the beginning of the next round when all workers return to their respective players.

Remember that players can use any conduits, mines, or tree farms they choose; it does not matter which player built it. It is the builder, though, who receives the points.

Customize It!

New Workforce. Try designing some new workers with different abilities. Perhaps there's a supremely efficient robot that can double the production of your current robots, delivering two resources every time you place them on a mine instead of only one. They could even provide a resource from a different mine than the one they're placed on. Try to think about what trait or ability might improve the game, and design a worker to accommodate.

Excavation Expansion. If it feels like the map is too small for your big dig, or that the number of players crowds the board, create a giant board. It could follow the same design but allow for longer connections and more tree farms.

This could provide space for a new type of building or resource as well. Similar to the UV robots and the tree farms, these new buildings or resources could be gated behind a player's progress.

For example, players can build water treatment facilities that extend beyond tree farms, by first building a tree farm and then extending conduits to reach the facility. This new building could provide the resource of a Gallon of Pure Water worth 1 point each—necessary for terraforming the planet.

Take it a step further and create the resource of a Tree, worth 5 points each, which would require a Sapling and 2 Gallons of Pure Water to create, warranting another space on the board to "build" the Tree.

Hovels & Hydras

30-60 MINUTES **2-7 PLAYERS** **AGES 11+**

Hovels & Hydras celebrates the transition from old wargames to modern RPGs. It demonstrates how a traditional checkered game board can morph into a thematic gridded map, and simple game pieces into characters with unique stats and traits.

A party of Heroes makes its way through a dungeon in the hope of slaying the Monsters. Two players can make the adventure a head-to-head competition (each controlling an opposing group), or many can play as teams (communicating with their allies and taking down the opponent). Either way, it's essential to understand all of the qualities of the characters you will be controlling.

COMPONENTS

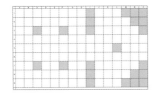

BOARD

Gridded dungeon

GAME PIECES

Parties of 4 Heroes and 3 Monsters

DIE/PAPER & A HAT

1 d20 or numbered slips of paper

x10

CARDS

Character cards & Deck of Discovery

TOKENS

Passed action tokens, wounded chits, and status counters

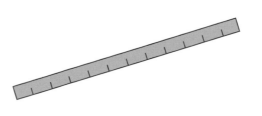

TOOLS

Ruler

INSTRUCTIONS

Rules

GOAL: Capture opponent's game pieces by striking multiple times and lowering their Toughness to 0.

PREP: Place game pieces in their starting positions, using the numbers and letters along the sides of the game board to find each spot.

Heroes: Berserker, A2; Fencer, A4; Spellcaster, A6; Archer, A8

Monsters: one Dölgin, I4; one Dölgin, I6; 3-Headed Hydra, O5.

Determine which players control which pieces. Players can divide control in any way they like. Each player may control any number of characters as long as they belong to the same party (Heroes or Monsters).

Lay out in front of you the character cards for the pieces you control, to remind you of each character's stats and powers. Set the different tokens into separate piles for players to access as needed. Lastly, shuffle the Deck of Discovery.

STARTING PLAYERS: The last person to visit a basement receives three action tokens to apply to any one character specifically. Another action token is given to any character within the opposing party.

GAME END: Once a party of characters has captured all of the opposing party's game pieces, the game is over, and that side wins (Heroes vs. Monsters).

TURN OVERVIEW: Once players begin taking action, paying attention is crucial. The passed action tokens create a sense of real-time play because turns are happening simultaneously. A player's character can move, attack, move-and-attack, or draw a card from the Deck of Discovery.

These actions have costs, and the tokens are used to pay them, then passed in a clockwise rotation to determine who the active characters are. Only pass an action token once an action has been completed.

You can choose to move-and-attack combined as one option. The benefit is that you do not have to pass any of the action tokens until after you complete the attack.

A player's character can draw a card. Each character has a hand limit of three cards, and each card is usable once. When cards are drawn, they apply only to that character. Positive cards can be added to their hand and played later. Negative cards are automatically applied to their next attack, then discarded. Turn rotation and actions strictly follow action token usage.

➡ To move costs 1 action token, attacking costs 2, and to move-and-attack costs 3. Moving and attacking are both impeded by walls, columns, and the opposing party's game pieces. Drawing a card from the deck of discovery costs 1 action token.

Steps

1. If a character is in possession of one or more action tokens, then they may take action.

2. After spending the action token(s) and completing a task, players pass the token(s) to the next character, which may be controlled by the very same player.

Exceptions & Explanations

Each character has movement patterns described on their cards that allow them to move up to a number of spaces. They don't have to move that total number, though. For example, the Fencer can move up to 5 spaces, but may move only 3.

When attempting to attack an opponent, characters are limited by their Range and must have a proper line of sight. Their Range is the maximum distance away that their target can be. The shaded spaces on the board denote walls and columns, meaning that they impede a character's attack and movement. Use a ruler if the line of sight is in question. Line of sight is discussed further in reference to movement.

FLIP to pg. 41 for more info!

To land an attack, roll a 20-sided die (d20). Add the attacker's Chance value to the result. If the number is equal to or higher than the opposing character's Target Value, then the attack is successful (stat check resolution).

To deal damage, set wounded chits enough to equal the attacking character's Power on top of the target character's card. The status counter is used only in the Archer's attack. Place it on the target character's card to show that their Chance is reduced for one turn.

The number inside the gem at the top of each card is the character's Toughness. The number at the top right is their Target Value.

Customize It!

Terrain Change. A simple modification could be to alter some of the spaces. Perhaps there are areas with jagged rocks strewn about; this alteration could affect a game piece by dealing damage or abruptly stopping its movement. These unfavorable locations could limit players to moving only one space at a time until they reach standard spaces.

In contrast you could also provide favorable spaces that project players forward an additional space, like a stream of water or gust of wind. Or, simply add more walls that limit the force projection of characters and make it more challenging to set up long-range attacks with a line of sight.

Level Up. You could provide upgrade cards for each character. Characters could gain experience tokens each time they capture an opposing character, and once they earn two, they could trade them in to receive their upgrade cards, which have improved stats or abilities. To determine who gets the experience tokens after multiple strikes, employ the kill-steal mechanism. Additionally, your Heroes and Monsters could go on to a new board of your own creation . . . expanding their world.

Further Discovery. Add new cards to the Deck of Discovery. You could provide more ways of healing or strengthening a character's Power. You could even include permanent cards instead of only one-time use cards. They could represent armor or weapons that your character wears throughout the game.

ACKNOWLEDGMENTS

I sincerely appreciate the faith, encouragement, and support that have provided the confidence for my creativity to flow freely. Thank you to my high school and community college art teacher, Bonnie Tatro Capogna. Thank you to my university professor and academic advisor, Patricia Galvis Assmus. Thank you to my executive consultant, editor, and wife, Jaclyn Gladstein.

Thank you to my additional editors and prototype testers: Colin Tincknell, Jordan and Lauren Imhoff, Pat Rogers, Kate Gladstein, Scott, Hayden, and Jordan Witt, Stephanie Wong, Zach and Grace Moses, and Lexi Girard.

Thank you to those who supported the success of my company Pied Raven Games and my first published tabletop game, Hibernation: Trevor Daniels, Karen and Matt Cimini, Shelly and Marty Gladstein, Michael Lampro, Julie Chee Perry, Rosalee Lampro, and John Daniels. Without Hibernation, I would not be here.

Additionally, thank you to those who playtested my games from the oldest to most current, soundboarded ideas, and gamed with me through the years: Sean Watroba, Bryan and Eric Fitzgerald, Brandon Daniels, Jake Girard, Jonathan and Kristina Maack, and Chris McCaul.

INDEX

A number in **pink** identifies the page where a term is defined.

DUELY NOTED COMPONENTS

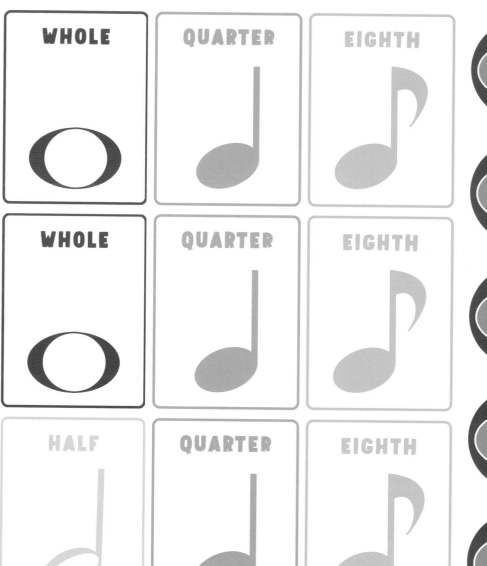

▲ TOKENS
5 victory points

◄ CARDS
You will need to create
4 whole notes, 8 half
notes, 10 quarter notes,
and 12 eighth notes.

Components

134

RAIN TOADS COMPONENTS

CARDS

You will need to create an event deck of 15 Sun and 5 Rain cards.

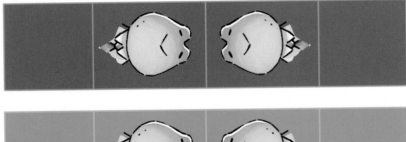

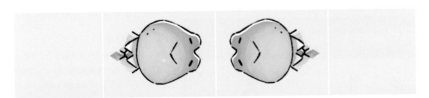
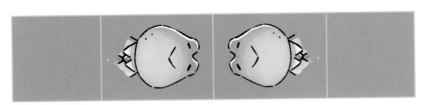

GAME PIECES
4 toads

CURRENCY
You will need
to create
30 Croak Coins.

INTERGALACTIC LABORATORY COMPONENTS

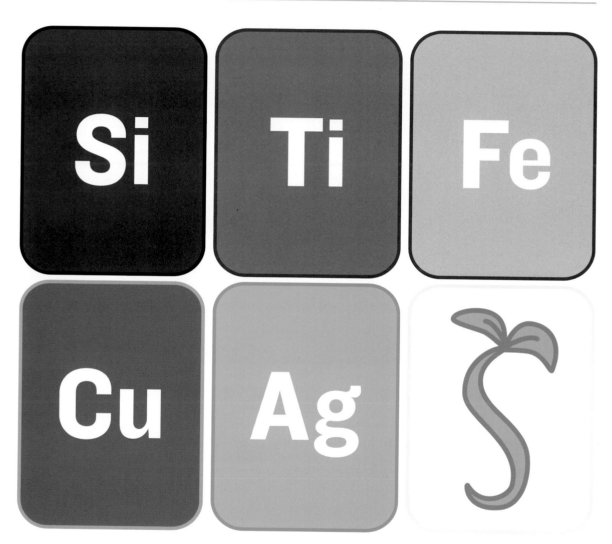

Si Ti Fe

Cu Ag

REFERENCE CARD

Silicon X 1
Silver X 1

Iron X 1
Copper X 2
Titanium X 2

Silicon X 2
Silver X 2
Iron X 2

Copper X 2
Titanium X 2

Silicon X 1   Copper X 1
Iron X 1   Silver X 2

Silicon X 1   Titanium X 1
Iron X 1   Robot X 1

▲ CARDS
You will need to create 5 unique resource card decks and a sapling card deck—7 of each card in each deck (create more as needed).

◄ PROP
Reference card

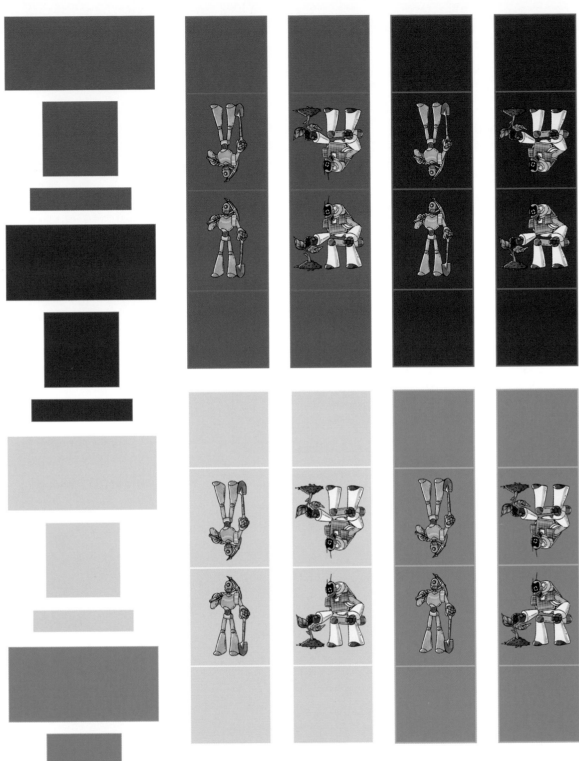

▲ GAME PIECES
You will need to create 4 uniquely colored sets of 7 robot workers and 4 UV robot workers.

◀ TOKENS
You will need to create 4 uniquely colored sets of 12 conduits, 6 mines, and 4 tree farms.

HOVELS & HYDRAS COMPONENTS

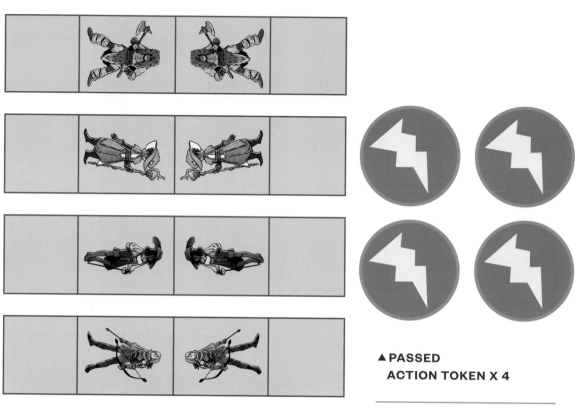

▲ PASSED
ACTION TOKEN X 4

▼ STATUS COUNTERS X 3

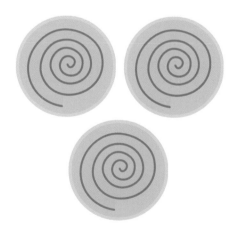

▲ GAME PIECES
Parties of 4 Heroes and 3 Monsters

Berserker

Gem: 4 **Target:** 8

MOVE up to 5 spaces horizontally or vertically

ATTACK if successful, push target 1 space in any direction

0 Chance **1** Range **1** Power

Spellcaster

Gem: 3 **Target:** 7

MOVE up to 1 space horizontally or vertically, then up to 1 diagonally

ATTACK if there is another opponent within 4 spaces of target, they're also attacked

0 Chance **4** Range **1** Power

Fencer

Gem: 3 **Target:** 8

MOVE up to 5 spaces diagonally

ATTACK if adjacent to an ally, then gain +2 chance

0 Chance **1** Range **1** Power

▲ WOUNDED CHITS X 10   ▲ CHARACTER CARDS

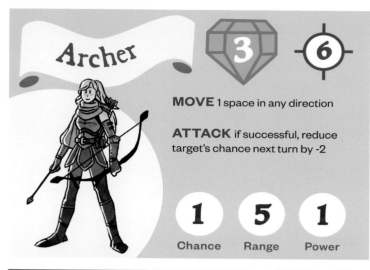

Archer

3 💎   **6** ⊙

MOVE 1 space in any direction

ATTACK if successful, reduce target's chance next turn by -2

1	**5**	**1**
Chance	Range	Power

Dölgin

3 💎   **10** ⊙

MOVE 2 spaces horizontally or vertically, then up to 2 diagonally

ATTACK if there is another opponent within 4 spaces of target, they're also attacked

1	**5**	**1**
Chance	Range	Power

3-Headed Hydra

4 💎   **13** ⊙

MOVE 1 space in any direction

ATTACK 3 times per attack

1	**5**	**1**
Chance	Range	Power

▲ CHARACTER CARDS

▶ DECK OF DISCOVERY CARDS
You will need 10 cards.

Components

+2 CHANCE

+2 CHANCE

−2 CHANCE

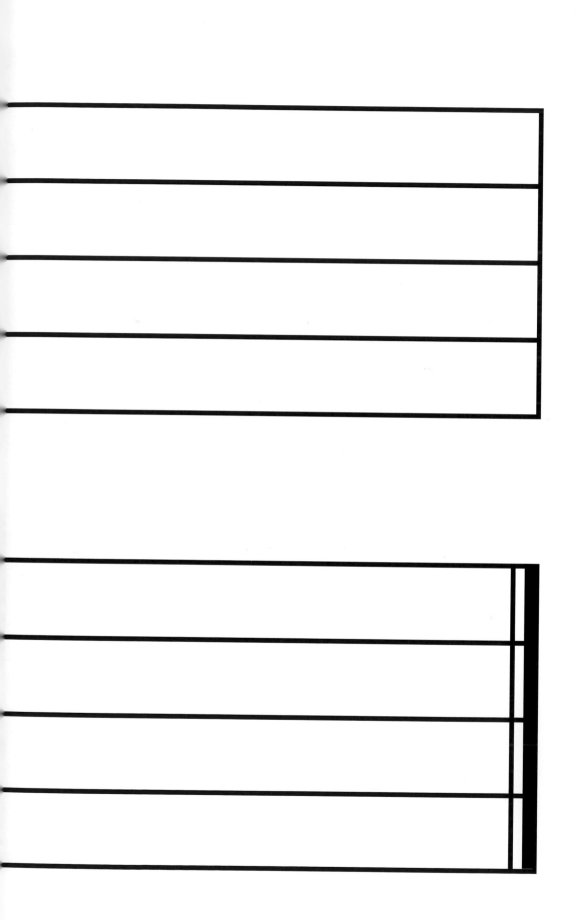

H	I	J	K	L	M	N	O
	▓				▓	▓	▓
	▓					▓	▓
	▓						▓
				▓			
	▓						▓
	▓					▓	▓
	▓				▓	▓	▓

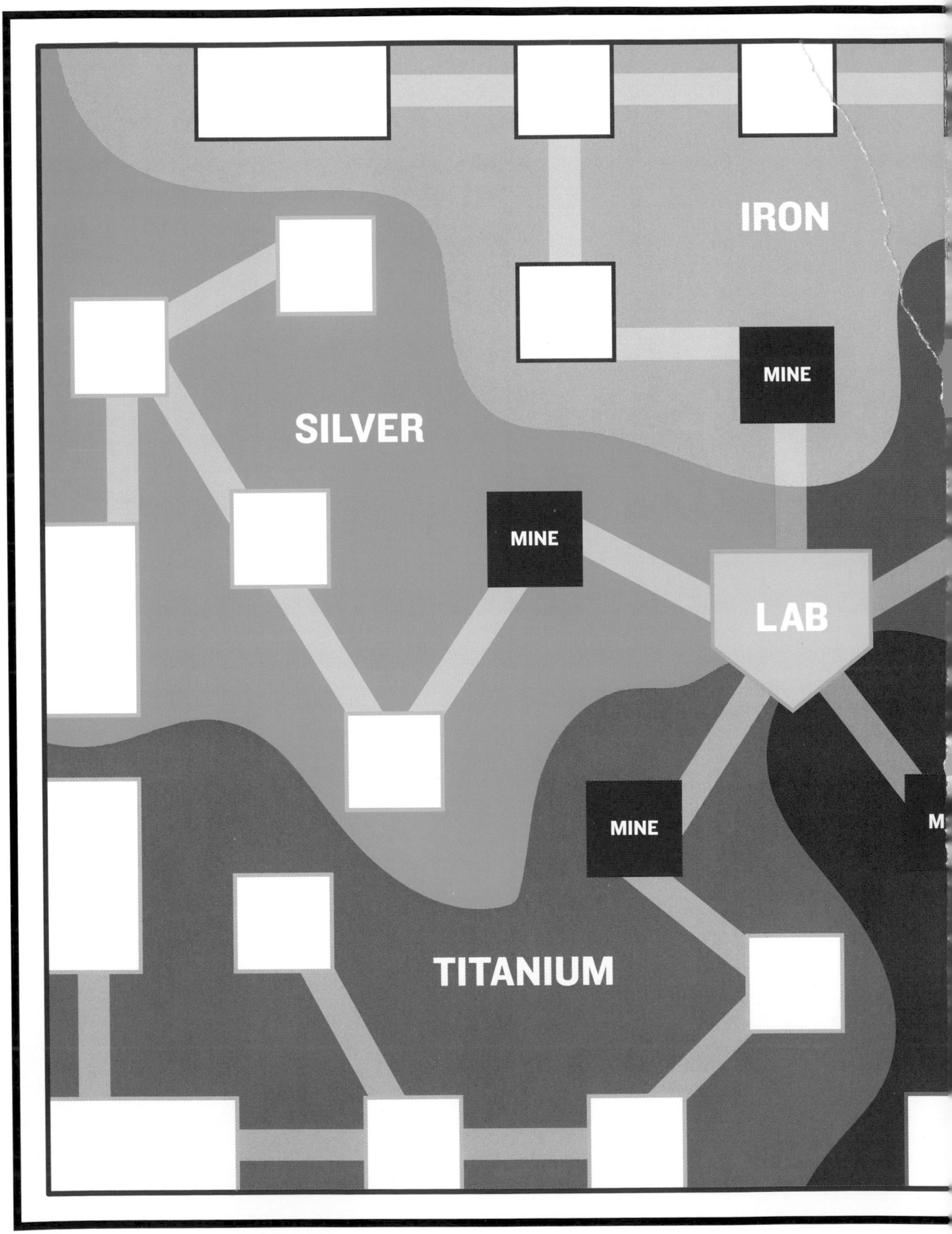

IRON

SILVER

MINE

MINE

LAB

MINE

M

TITANIUM

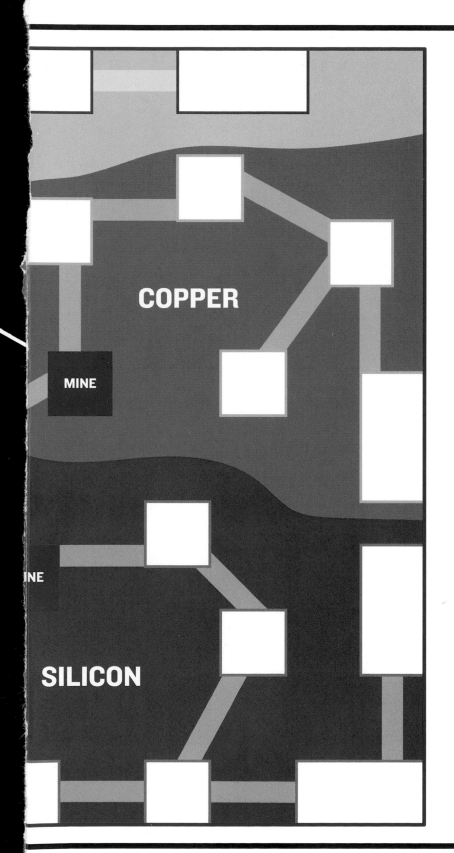

Build a conduit

Build a mine

Build a tree farm

Go 1st next round

	A	B	C	D	E	F	G	
1								
2								
3								
4								
5								
6								
7								
8								
9								